SCHOLASTIC

Teaching With Favorite
READ-ALOUDS
— in Second Grade —

**50 Must-Have Books With Lessons and Activities
That Build Skills in Vocabulary, Comprehension,
and More**

By Susan Lunsford

New York • Toronto • London • Auckland • Sydney
Mexico City • New Delhi • Hong Kong • Buenos Aires

Teaching
Resources

DEDICATION

For Ryan & Maddie
And all the children who helped me with this book. Keep your love of books forever!

To Brad & Margo:
Your support was a must-have for this book of Must-Have Read-Alouds.

For Tara and her amazing second graders::
Your smiles and hard work have made this book extra special!

For Joanna and Sarah:
Thanks for your guidance and support.

Cover design by Josuè Castilleja
Cover photograph by Jon Freilich/Getty
Interior Design by LDL Designs, based on a design by Sarah Morrow
Interior illustrations by Sharon Holm

ISBN 0-439-40419-3

Printed in the U.S.A.

4 5 6 7 8 9 10   40   10 09 08 07

CONTENTS

Stock Your Bookshelf With Tempting Must-Have Books

I was a second grader long before the days of videos, DVDs, and television channels that go above 100. My children find it hard to believe I survived such a barbaric beginning. "You mean you only had four channels?" my son asks in disbelief. "Yes. It was wonderful," I answer as I turn off the television.

I had a bookshelf stocked with books. And a back-yard where my best friend and I spent many memorable days, ice skating in winter and riding bikes in summer. When we needed a break, we would grab matching copies of books to read together. *Alexander and the Terrible, Horrible, No Good, Very Bad Day, Ira Sleeps Over,* and *Frog and Toad Together* were new in 1972 when I was in second grade. Susan and I (yes, her name is Susan, too) sat together under the oak tree in my yard or the willow tree in hers and read. We didn't need a remote, or a VCR, all we needed were matching copies from our schoolbook orders or the library. Now, pushing forty, we are reading these same stories to our kids. The same books we loved as children are turning our children into readers, too.

Susi and Susan, September 1972: The author (on the right) and her best friend on the first day of second grade

Read-aloud is the most important part of the school day for impressing second graders with just how entertaining books can be. With every read-aloud, you are instilling a love of literature and providing motivation to learn to read and to keep reading for a lifetime. Sure, there will always be children who choose television over books, but most second graders are equally impressed with the tempting books written by the impressive array of authors featured in this book of must-haves.

So find the must-have books in the pages that follow. Read them aloud with your second graders for pure entertainment value. Then revisit the

Ryan, Mommy, and Maddie, September 2002: The author and her children hear *Frog and Toad*

books to link the learning of skills to a favorite character, idea, theme, or words taken from their pages. Experiment with the mini-lessons and activities in this book and adapt them to suit your students' needs and your teaching style. Use some lessons and activities for your whole class and others for small-group instruction, or stretch some of them over the course of several days. However you present the ideas in this book, my hope is that together you and your students will enjoy a year of book-based learning.

The author's friend Susan reading to her children, Sarah and Rachel

Share the 50 must-have books on the following pages with the second graders in your life. Sure, they'll probably grow up to love television, videos, and DVDs, but hopefully, years from now, there may be a few well-loved picture books from second grade on the shelf with the favorite movies, just waiting to be shared with their children someday, too.

A Few Words About the Read-Aloud and Rich Vocabulary Connection

It's no surprise that by their senior year, students at the top of their class know about four times as many words as their lower performing classmates. "Most chilling, however," write Beck, McKeown, and Kucan in *Bringing Words to Life* (pages 1–2), "is the finding that once established, such differences appear difficult to ameliorate. This is clearly very bad news!"

The good news is that implementing effective vocabulary instruction has become a priority in elementary schools. Techniques for providing the most effective and meaningful vocabulary instruction have also been identified. For second-grade teachers, the most appropriate place to begin is with a daily read-aloud, which gives the opportunity to teach one or two new words. Read-aloud time will provide a wealth of vocabulary words in meaningful contexts over the course of the school year.

In the pages of my book, I highlight one or more words from each of the 50 must-have read-aloud books. Activities and direct examples from my classroom illustrate how to best present words from trade books to help second graders commit new word knowledge to memory and to apply these newly discovered words in new situations.

Chapter 1:
Animal Character Studies
10 Must-Have Books for Word Study and Spelling Practice

Chapter Learning Goals:

* using conventions of spelling in written compositions
* identifying spelling patterns
* using writing to describe familiar situations and events
* incorporating descriptive language into written compositions
* incorporating conventions of capitalization and punctuation in written compositions
* understanding book-related vocabulary
* using various strategies to decode unknown words
* enjoying great books with animal characters

A wishful donkey, two hilarious hippos, bunnies who bake cakes, a crocodile who helps with homework, a runaway dog, and an odd penguin are just a few of the animal characters who make studying words meaningful and motivating in this chapter of must-have read-alouds. Share each book for read-aloud, and then use the words and themes featuring these favorite animal characters to reinforce phonemic and conventional spelling, the mechanics of writing, and vocabulary.

Challenge students to find all 70 *-ed* words in *Sylvester and the Magic Pebble*. Use phonemic writing to compile a list of pros and cons for moving with *Town Mouse, Country Mouse*, make a shopping list for Max and Ruby in *Bunny Cakes*, and a list of things to take to *Arthur's First Sleepover*. Hone capitalization and punctuation with sentences from *George and Martha*. Identify short vowel words used to tell the story of *Tacky the Penguin*. Use appropriate vocabulary words to complete a story based on *Chester's Way*. Go on a hunt for words beginning with *r*-blends with *Lyle, Lyle Crocodile*, and then classify long vowel words in *The Great Gracie Chase*. Prove the power of adjectives with *Fritz and the Mess Fairy*.

Grab copies of these 10 must-have books to give your students a better understanding of how the world of words works.

10 Must-Have Books for Word Study and Spelling Practice

Sylvester and the Magic Pebble by William Steig

Town Mouse, Country Mouse by Jan Brett

George and Martha: The Complete Stories of Two Best Friends by James Marshall

Bunny Cakes by Rosemary Wells

Arthur's First Sleepover by Marc Brown

Tacky the Penguin by Helen Lester

Chester's Way by Kevin Henkes

Lyle, Lyle, Crocodile by Bernard Waber

The Great Gracie Chase: Stop That Dog by Cynthia Rylant

Fritz and the Mess Fairy by Rosemary Wells

Sylvester and the Magic Pebble

by William Steig

LEARNING ABOUT Word Endings

Sylvester Duncan lived with his mother and father at Acorn Road in Oatsdale. One of his hobbies was collecting pebbles of unusual shape and color.
— From *Sylvester and the Magic Pebble*, page 3

Sylvester shivers with excitement when he finds a perfectly round, shiny, red pebble that grants his every wish. Unfortunately, when a mean and hungry lion approaches and Sylvester wishes he were a rock, this wish comes true. What kind of magic will turn Sylvester back into his former donkey self? Just the right amount of suspense, humor, and a happy ending make this a favorite book for young readers. William Steig's fluent text makes this a perfect book for studying words with *-ed* and *-ing* endings and building vocabulary.

For a fun, book-based lesson that helps students appreciate the variety of words William Steig uses to tell his story, mark unusual pebbles (real or made from paper or clay) with *-ed* words from the story. Place the pebbles in a glass jar, just like Sylvester did on the opening page. Record one of the words from the story (shown in their order of appearance on page 9) on a pebble for each student. (For 20 students, copy the first 20 words.) Ask students to hold up their pebbles when they hear an *—ed* word as you reread *Sylvester and the Magic Pebble* and then match the corresponding pebble to the word. Supply a donkey shape cut from colored paper for students to make tally marks of the *-ed* word in the story. Record the words on a chart as students identify them.

Note: Some *-ed* words are repeated in the story. The numbers in parentheses reflect the number of times a word is repeated.

Rich Vocabulary

remarkable *adj.*
not ordinary

-ed Words from *Sylvester and the Magic Pebble*

lived, stopped, ceased, vanished, disappeared, existed, gratified, guessed, happened (4), turned, wished (5), started, startled, frightened (2), panicked, sniffed (3), walked (2), confused, perplexed, puzzled, bewildered, muttered, scared, worried, imagined, realized (2), paced, stayed (2), cried, longed, talked, smelled, concluded, tried (2), included, reminded, followed (3), used, snowed, stared, howled (2), melted, warmed, budded, showed, insisted, wanted (3), loved, looked (2), calmed

My collection of -*ed* word pebbles

Here's how the activity works in my classroom.

Luke:	What's in the jar?
Mrs. L.:	My collection of pebbles to share with you.
Maggie:	Just like Sylvester's.
Timothy:	Did you bring any magic pebbles?
Mrs. L.:	We'll soon find out. I'd like each of you to choose a pebble from the jar.
Annie:	Hey, this pebble has a word on it.
George:	So does mine!
Mrs. L.:	Hold up your pebbles. Look at the words on these magic pebbles. What do all the words have in common?
Matthew:	They're words from the story.
Jan:	Yes, and they all have *e-d* at the end.
Amanda:	My word is *walked*. That's what Sylvester did.
Jesse:	Oh—they're all doing words.
Mrs. L.:	*Walk, sniff, talk,* and *wish,* for example, are all action words. Action words are called verbs. When you add -*ed* to a verb, the action happened in the past.
Luke:	So *walk* would turn into *walked*.
Mrs. L:	That's right. Let's reread *Sylvester and the Magic Pebble*. Hold up your magic pebble when you hear a word that ends in -*ed*. We'll identify each word. Then you'll place your matching pebble on the chalkboard ledge and make a tally mark on the donkey to help us keep track of the -*ed* words in the story. I'll write the words on a chart. Here's the first page: "Sylvester Duncan lived with his mother and father"—You're holding up your magic pebbles to stop me. What -*ed* word did you hear?
Class:	*Lived!*
Mrs. L.:	Look at all the pebbles. Who has the pebble with *lived* on it?
Michael:	I have *lived!*
Mrs. L.:	Michael, please put your pebble on the chalkboard ledge. Then make a tally mark on the donkey. *(I write* lived *on the chart.)*

Mrs. L.:	If I cover the *-ed,* what's left?
Class:	*L-i-v.*
Mrs. L.:	The root word *live* ends in a silent *e.* So when you want to say, "Sylvester lived in Oatsdale," you only need to add a *d* since *live* already ends in *e*. *(I read the story in its entirety. The discussion below highlights some sentences with -ed words and their different spelling rules.)*
Mrs. L.:	"To his great surprise the rain stopped"—
Class:	*Stopped!*
Dean:	I have *stopped.*
Mrs. L.:	Take off the *-ed* and you have—
Dean:	*Stop! S-t-o-p-p.* Is there an extra *p?*
Mrs. L.:	Some words need an extra letter before the *-ed* is added. If you want to write *stop,* it's *s-t-o-p.* If you want to write *stopped,* you add a *p* before adding *e-d.* We'll see if William Steig used any more of these special words. *(I continue to read.)*
Class:	*Ceased!*
Mrs. L.:	What does *ceased* mean?
Allison:	The same as *stopped. Ceased* is my word. When you take off the *-ed, c-e-a-s* is left. That's *cease.*
Mrs. L.:	Nice reading. *Cease* is another word with a silent *e* so you only need to add a *d* to this word to show the rain stopped or ceased. I'm going to ask you to wait until I've finished reading the next sentence. Count on your fingers the number of *-ed* words you hear in this sentence: "The drops vanished on the way down, the clouds disappeared, everything was dry, and the sun was shining as if rain had never existed."
Class:	Three!
Luke:	I have a *v* word. It's *vanished.*
Mrs. L.:	Take off the *-ed* and what's left?
Luke:	*Vanish. V-a-n-i-s-h.*
Mrs. L.:	There is a word in the sentence that means the same as *vanished.*
Hannah:	*Disappeared.* That's my word. *D-i-s-a-p-p-e-a-r* with *-ed.* That's our fifth tally.
Mrs. L.:	I see one more *-ed* word in that sentence.
Annie:	*Existed.* Jan has that one.
Jan:	I'll put it on the ledge.
Mrs. L.:	Let's keep reading: "In all his young life Sylvester had never had a wish gratified so quickly."
Class:	Stop!
Sydney:	You said *gratified.*
David:	It's my word, I think. It starts with *g-r.*
Mrs. L.:	That's right. Listen to the sentence again, and tell me what you think *gratified* means: "In all his young life Sylvester had never had a wish gratified so quickly."
Sydney:	*Granted.* His wish was granted. *Gratified* sounds fancier than *granted.*
Mrs. L.:	William Steig is an expert at using fancy words, isn't he? Let's take the *-ed* off *gratified.* What's left?

David:	*Gratify.*
Mrs. L.:	You've got it. Spell the root word.
Class:	*G-r-a-t-i-f-i.*
Mrs. L.:	Close. There's a spelling rule for words like *gratify*. The last letter of the root word *gratify* is *y*. *G-r-a-t-i-f-y* spells *gratify*. The *y* changes to an *i* before you add *-ed*. Say this with me.
Class:	*Y* changes to *i* before you add *-ed*.
Mrs. L.:	Nice job! Back to the story: "It struck him that magic must be at work, and he guessed that the magic"—
Class:	*Guessed.*
Mrs. L.:	Good listening. Look around. Guess who has the word *guessed*.
Abby:	Jake does!
Jake:	I guess I do!
Mrs. L.:	Take off the *-ed* and you have—
Jake:	*Guess. G-u-e-s-s.*
Mrs. L.:	No spelling rules there. You just add the *-ed*. I'll keep reading: "I wish it would rain again. Nothing happened."
Class:	*Happened*!
Maggie:	I have it! *Happen* is what's left when you take off the *-ed*.
Mrs. L.:	Right! "But when he said the same thing holding the pebble in his hoof, the sky turned black"—
Timothy:	Stop! I have that one. The word is *turned*. Cover up the *–ed*, and it's *turn*. (*We continue reading the next three pages and record five tally marks for* wished, *two for* frightened, *and one each for* started, startled, *and* panicked. *Our mini-lesson continues as Sylvester turns into a rock on Strawberry Hill.*)
Mrs. L.:	"'I wish I were a rock,' he said, and he became a rock." Now listen to the next two sentences without stopping me. Count on your fingers the number of *-ed* words you hear. "The lion came bounding over, sniffed the rock a hundred times, walked around and around it, and went away confused, perplexed, puzzled and bewildered. 'I saw that little donkey as clear as day. Maybe I'm going crazy,' he muttered."
Carrie:	Six.
Kristen:	No, seven!
Mrs. L.:	Smile if you counted seven *-ed* words in that sentence!
Maggie:	They were fancy ones, too.
Mrs. L.:	I'll read the paragraph again slowly. Hold up your pebbles to stop me so we can identify the seven tricky *-ed* words: "The lion came bounding over, sniffed the rock a hundred times"—
Chris:	*Sniffed* is my word. Does *sniff* have an extra *f*?
Mrs. L.:	No, but I can see why you might think so. *Stopped* did have an extra *p*. *Sniff* is spelled *s-n-i-f-f*. Here's the rest of that sentence: "walked around"—
Amanda:	Stop! I have *walked*.
Mrs. L.:	Great. "The lion walked around and around it, and went away confused"—

David:	Stop! My pebble has *confused* on it. Take the *-ed* off, and you have *c-o-n-f-u-s*.
Mrs. L.:	*Confuse* ends in a silent *e* so you only—
David:	Add a *d*.
Mrs. L.:	Right. I'll keep reading: "perplexed, puzzled and bewildered."
Class:	Stop! Stop! Stop!
Jenny:	He's really confused. Sylvester really tricked him. All those words mean "confused or tricked," don't they?
Mrs. L.:	Yes. Let's add these pebbles to the chalkboard ledge.
Jenny:	I think I have one of them. *P-e-r-p-l-e-x-e-d* is on my rock.
Michael:	That's *perplexed*.
Joel:	I have *bewildered*.
Mrs. L.:	*Bewildered*. Good.
Jesse:	I've got the last pebble.
Mrs. L.:	I'll read the next thing the lion says: "'I saw that little donkey as clear as day. Maybe I'm going crazy,' he muttered."
Jesse:	My word is *muttered*.
Luke:	That must be all the *-ed* words there are in the story.
Allison:	I bet there are more than that. The story isn't over yet.

Throughout the day, we continue reading and writing the remaining *-ed* words in *Sylvester and the Magic Pebble.* To the students' surprise, they find that William Steig used a total of 70 words with the *-ed* ending in his story. The importance of this special verb ending is proven meaningful.

ON ANOTHER DAY

We organize the words by the unique spelling rules used.

Just add *-ed* to these words

existed	happened	turned	wished	frightened	sniffed
bewildered	stayed	walked	panicked★	perplexed	guessed
muttered	longed	talked	disappeared	vanished	smelled
reminded	followed	snowed	howled	melted	warmed
showed	insisted	wanted	looked	calmed	

★ Add a *k* and then *−ed*.

Just add *-d* to words that end in silent *e*

lived	ceased	startled	confused	puzzled	scared
imagined	concluded	realized	paced	used	stored
included	loved				

Double the final consonant and then add *-ed*

stopped   budded

Change *y* to *i* and then add *-ed*

gratified	worried	cried	tried

More Must-Have Books
For Word Study and Spelling Practice

....

Town Mouse, Country Mouse
by Jan Brett

LEARNING ABOUT

Reinforcing Spelling

"This is the life! Wildflowers, spring peepers. If only we lived here!"
The country mice crept out. "You like it here?" they asked. "Why, we've always wanted to live in a town house."
The town mouse offered them a nibble of cheese. "Why don't we trade houses?" he said.
— From *Town Mouse, Country Mouse*, page 7

What happens when two town mice trade homes with two country mice? They come to the understanding that there's no place like home. In this classic tale beautifully retold and illustrated by Jan Brett, the pictures beg to be pored over so readers can take in the multitude of details. The beaded and bejeweled outfits worn by the town mouse wife and the town mouse husband's too bright red jacket attract the attention of a curious blackbird. The humble country mice wear a straw hat and a babushka, and you get the uncanny feeling that the hungry cat in a flowered tapestry vest might jump right out of the book in its search for them. This book is a favorite of second graders.

Last spring, as I prepared myself for a possible move from town to country, I related to the feelings experienced by the mice in this book. It wasn't as easy as switching keys and moving in; I had to weigh the options and accept that some lifestyle changes would be required. But unlike the town mice, my husband and I made a list of pros and cons for our family's move from town to the country. When I wrote down *no pizza delivery* under cons, my husband suggested this could be a pro—our pizza delivery savings could pay for our son's college education (ha ha).

It occurred to me that pretending to be town mice preparing for a permanent move to the country would generate thoughtful discussions among my second graders. After rereading the story, I asked my students to help me complete a pros-and-cons list on which the town and country mice could base their decisions to move or to stay.

We began with the town mice. Students recorded their ideas on a chart by using sound-spelling. Together, we recorded the main sounds in the words as shown. Endings, blends, and vowel sounds

Rich Vocabulary

exclaimed *v.* said in an excited voice

envy *v.* to want something that belongs to another

were reinforced with meaningful spelling practice. Students gave more reasons for staying in town; like the mice, they felt that there was no place like home.

Moving from Town to the Country

Advantages:
- fresh air, wildflowers
- no cat prowling the house
- quiet and peaceful life
- wild blackberries for every meal
- no dangerous attempts to reach food in the pantry
- beautiful scenery
- no more mousetraps

Disadvantages:
- getting caught in storms while searching for food
- nearly getting carried away by a curious blackbird
- cannot wear brightly colored clothes
- miss the sounds of town, the hustle and bustle
- no more smell of cheese to make whiskers tingle
- feeling alone
- cats with wings (owls)
- not knowing what to expect in a new place
- lots of different dangerous animals to avoid

ON ANOTHER DAY

Have small groups work on a similar list of advantages and disadvantages to help the country mice decide whether or not to move into town.

Note: My family and I realized we were town mice at heart. We are happily settled in a new town house, not a country house.

....

George and Martha:
The Complete Stories of Two Best Friends
by James Marshall

LEARNING ABOUT

Capitalization and Punctuation

In his touching foreword to this book, Maurice Sendak describes James Marshall as someone who "raised the art of friendship to a new height." Marshall's two comical hippos, George and Martha, can teach children a thing or two about friendship; through jokes, jobs, birthdays, picnics and scary movies, George and Martha are best friends.

Marshall's simple sketches, his use of color, and compelling squiggly line eyes bring these two characters to life. *George and Martha: The Complete Stories of Two Best Friends* is a 25th-anniversary anthology that includes all seven George and Martha books. Each of the seven books contains five vignettes for a total of 35 stories. These books are also in print individually: *George and Martha* (1972), *George and Martha Encore* (1973), *George and Martha Rise and Shine* (1976), *George and Martha One Fine Day* (1978), *George and Martha Tons of Fun* (1980), *George and Martha Back in Town* (1984), and *George and Martha Round and Round* (1988).

Share any George and Martha book for a read-aloud, and students will become instant fans. Let the antics of these two hilarious hippos energize a few lessons on capitalization and punctuation. Write two sets of sentences from *George and Martha Back in Town*. Use one set to introduce the capitalization of proper nouns and the first letters of sentences. Discuss the proper placement of periods, exclamation points, and commas after a series of words.

> **Add missing capital letters, periods (.), exclamation marks (!), and commas (,) to these sentences from George and Martha Back in Town.**
>
> 1. martha noticed a little box on george's kitchen table
> 2. out jumped george's entire collection of mexican jumping beans
> 3. martha bit her nails while george pulled off the ribbon
> 4. out jumped one rubber tarantula one stuffed snake four plastic spiders and two real frogs
> 5. everyone was impressed
> 6. but soon martha was fidgeting

Use the other set of sentences to have students put quotation marks around the words that George and Martha say to each other. For an added challenge, ask students to identify which of the five short stories each sentence is from: "The Box," "The High Board," "The Trick," "The Job," or "The Book."

> **Add the missing quotation marks (" ") to these sentences from George and Martha Back in Town.**
>
> 1. Oh my stars, said Martha.
> 2. I'm not the nosy type, said Martha.
> 3. Egads! cried George. I've been tricked!
> 4. I just didn't feel like it today, said George.
> 5. This will butter her up, he said.
> 6. No horsing around! he called through his megaphone.

MORE FUN WITH THE BOOK

After reading *George and Martha: The Complete Stories of Two Best Friends,* challenge students to write complete sentences using capitalization and punctuation to answer the following trivia questions about the book. Reread the short stories (in parentheses) as students check their trivia answers.

George and Martha Trivia Questions

1. What did George do to Martha's mirror? Why did he do it? ("The Mirror")
2. How did George get a gold tooth? ("The Tooth")
3. What are Martha's favorite flowers? ("The Garden")
4. Did Martha get back at George for squirting her with the hose? ("The Surprise")
5. What did Martha buy George for his birthday? What happened to this gift? What did George really get for his birthday? ("The Special Gift")
6. What did George buy Martha for her birthday? What did Martha do with this present? ("The Special Gift")
7. Who was the "touchy" artist? ("The Artist")
8. Why did George want to hypnotize Martha? ("The Hypnotist")
9. What did Martha do to get George to cut down on his sweets? ("The Sweet Tooth")
10. Where did George and Martha go on their trip? ("The Trip")

> ## TEACHING TIP
>
> To make assessment and recording words during word-study lessons more fun, provide students with paper cut in different shapes related to the story. Trace a simple shape onto a blank sheet of paper and cut multiple copies so each student can have one or two shapes. Banana shapes work well with the grocery-list activity for *Bunny Cakes*; flashlight shapes are fun to use with *Arthur's Sleepover*; and crocodile shapes are perfect to use with *Lyle, Lyle Crocodile*.

Bunny Cakes
by Rosemary Wells

LEARNING ABOUT

Reinforcing Book-Spelling

It was Grandma's birthday. Max made her an earthworm birthday cake.
"No, Max," said Max's sister, Ruby. "We are going to make Grandma an angel surprise cake with raspberry-fluff icing."

— From *Bunny Cakes*, page 3

Rich Vocabulary

eagerly *adv.* with excitement

Poor Max. His kitchen mishaps lead to four different trips to the grocery store so his older and rather bossy sister, Ruby, can complete Grandma's angel surprise birthday cake with raspberry-fluff icing. What Max really wants is some red-hot marshmallow squirters for the earthworm cake with caterpillar icing he is making for Grandma.

Unfortunately, the grocer can't read the words Max has added to Ruby's lists. But Max's persistence pays off. When the "most beautiful writing he knew" doesn't get results, he draws a picture of red-hot marshmallow squirters instead.

Share this must-have book featuring the sibling team of Max and Ruby for read-aloud while giving students some practical grocery list writing practice. Prior to the read-aloud, pass out paper for students to write their lists on (see the previous Teaching Tip), pencils, and lap boards. As you read the story, have students make a list of the items Ruby needs from the store. Encourage sound-spelling rather than copying the words from the illustrations.

Following the read-aloud, talk about how Ruby used book-spelling for her words and how Max's persistence resulted in a box of red-hot marshmallow squirters. On chart paper, demonstrate book-spelling for the words *milk, eggs, flour, birthday candles, sugar hearts,* and *buttercream roses.* Discuss conventions of spelling such as the following:

- consonant blends in *flour* and *cream*
- compound words (*birthday* and *buttercream*)
- long vowel patterns in *roses* and *cream*
- short vowel patterns in *milk, eggs, candles,* and *butter*

Mention that some words, like *sugar* and *hearts,* are exceptions to spelling rules; book-spelling for these words must be committed to memory. Have students check their lists for book-spelling and make any necessary corrections.

Discuss Max's attempts at "spelling" red-hot marshmallow squirters so that the grocer could decipher his "writing." Challenge pairs of students to add "red-hot marshmallow squirters" to their grocery lists using book-spelling. Instead of writing this on the class chart, provide spelling hints that guide students until they have achieved book-spelling for the words: "Think of *marshmallow* as a compound word. *Red* and *hot* are short vowel pattern words. *Squirters* is an *r*-controlled word." Students can be encouraged by Max's try-and-try-again attitude and meet with spelling success of their own.

....

Arthur's First Sleepover
by Marc Brown

**LEARNING
ABOUT**

Compound Words

Introduce *Arthur's First Sleepover* by asking, "Have you been to a sleepover?" After tallying the results, meet for a read-aloud of Arthur, Buster, and the Brain's first sleepover in Arthur's backyard tent. Read to find out if Arthur and his friends really do get any sleep at the sleepover, and if D.W. makes it into the *National Requirer* for seeing an alien.

Reread *Arthur's First Sleepover*, and ask students to stop you each time they hear a compound word. Marc Brown uses 12 compound words to tell this story: *sleepover, homework, breakfast, everyone, spaceship, bedtime, afternoon, cannonballs, outside, sleeptime, flashlight, baseball.*

ON ANOTHER DAY

For more practical list writing practice following the read-aloud, provide time for partners to write things they would need for a sleepover. Meet together for students to share their lists. As you chart the words in book-spelling, have students make changes to reflect this spelling. Highlight spelling conventions as illustrated in the sample list below:

Things Needed for a Sleepover

sleeping bag	pajamas
toothbrush	baseball cards or game
pillow	scary books
change of clothes	comb or brush
flashlight	slippers
Teddy bear	toothpaste

·····································

Tacky the Penguin
by Helen Lester

 **LEARNING ABOUT**   ## Short Vowel Sounds

There's something to be said about being your own person—or penguin! While the penguins Goodly, Lovely, Angel, Neatly, and Perfect march, dive, sing, and greet each other exactly the same way, Tacky has his own way of doing things. But when Tacky's fast thinking saves his companions and him, the other penguins develop a healthy respect for Tacky's odd ways and are thankful he's around.

Author and former second-grade teacher Helen Lester knows just what it takes to write a must-have book for this age group. "Read it again!" is the response shouted by my students every year when I share *Tacky the Penguin* as a read-aloud. Second graders giggle at Tacky's odd way of marching, his silly song about how many toes a fish has, and his splashy cannonball dives. Lynn Monsignor's comic portrayals of the companion penguins perfectly complement Helen Lester's rollicking text.

Tacky the Penguin has just the right amount of text per page for short vowel word practice. Identify *Tacky* as the short vowel *a* guide word. Discuss whether words such as *back, sat,* and *pack* have the same vowel sound as *Tacky*. Emphasize the short vowel sound by drawing out the *a*.

Following a read-aloud of the book, have students color and cut out a small drawing of Tacky on a 3-by-5-inch index card. They can tape the drawings to Popsicle sticks to make *Tacky the Penguin* puppets.

Then gather students for a rereading of the book. Ask them to flash their Tacky puppets each time they hear a short *a* word in the story. Students may copy the words onto a sheet of paper to reinforce spelling of short *a* words. You may also want to include a separate list of *r*-controlled and *n*-controlled vowel words found in the story.

Tacky words			*r*-controlled words	*n*-controlled words		
slap	maps	back	march(ed)	companions	ran	and
traps	happening	that's	dollar	distance	land	many
splashy	asked	have		an	hands	chanting
as	had	clasped		stand	cannonballs	

ON ANOTHER DAY
Reread *Tacky the Penguin* to identify short *e* and *i* words using the two syllables in *pen-guin* as a reference word.

························

Chester's Way
by Kevin Henkes

LEARNING ABOUT

Reinforcing Sound-Spelling

CHESTER had his own way of doing things . . .
He always cut his sandwiches diagonally.
He always got out of bed on the same side.
And he never left the house without double-knotting his shoes…
Chester's best friend Wilson was exactly the same way…
— From *Chester's Way*, pages 5–6, 8

Help students learn that three can be a crowd—of fun—based on this delightful story. Chester and Wilson are apprehensive when Lilly moves into

> **Rich Vocabulary**
>
> **original** *adj.* having your own way of doing things

the neighborhood. Then she saves them from some rude boys with one of her nifty disguises, and the three become inseparable. From raking leaves and wearing sunscreen to popping wheelies and double knotting their shoes, they do things their way.

For fun, have your students introduce themselves in a story that follows the pattern of Kevin Henkes's *Chester's Way*. Make copies of the reproducible on page 24. Have students complete the story using sound-spelling.

Provide time for sharing and discussing the similarities and differences among students. During this discussion, introduce the following vocabulary words from the story:

rude *adj.* without manners

nifty *adj.* neat, cool

inseparable *adj.* can't be without each other

disguised *v.* changed the way someone looks or sounds

Incorporate the words into descriptions such as the following:.

• Maggie's little brother can be rude.

• Carrie always wears nifty shoes.

• Sydney and Kristen are inseparable and play together all the time.

• To sound like his older brother, Matthew disguised his voice.

................Seth................'s Way
Based on *Chester's Way* by Kevin Henkes.
Hello, my name is _Seth_
I like _Hikes_ and _Kyler_ and _Connor_
I always _say chese hogie_
I never _like being sick_
For breakfast, I always have _candy_
I always carry with me _a door knob_ Just in case.
I love to go _climb a tree_
In spring I _eat_
In winter, I _play snow forts_
In fall, I _slide into leeves_
And in summer, I _cut with sisisors_
I definitely have my own way of doing things

Seth's Way

Lyle, Lyle, Crocodile
by Bernard Waber

LEARNING ABOUT Word Endings

Bernard Waber's crocodile, Lyle, has been entertaining young audiences since 1965. For Lyle fans, the idea of having a pet crocodile that sings, dances, and helps with homework is awesome. Lyle's family, the Primms, feels the same way. But Mr. Grumps and his cat Loretta who live two houses away are less than impressed with the Primms' unusual pet; in fact Lyle makes them miserable. So Mrs. Primm and her crocodile keep a low profile for awhile. Then Mr. Grumps makes good on a promise, and Lyle is sent to live at the zoo.

Read the story of *Lyle, Lyle Crocodile,* and pause at the page where Lyle is sprung from the zoo by Hector P. Valenti, star of stage and screen. Ask: "What can Lyle do to be welcomed by

Mr. Grumps as a neighbor again?" Discuss possible endings, and then read the rest of the story to check predictions. My second graders are always impressed with Bernard Waber's choice to have Lyle rescue Mr. Grumps and Loretta from their burning house.

Following the read aloud, use *Lyle, Lyle Crocodile* to assess students. Provide them with crocodile-shaped paper (see the Teaching Tip on page 16), and settle them in for a page-by-page rereading of the story. Prior to reading each page, ask a question such as the following to assess their understanding of word endings, capitalization, and more.

Assessing with *Lyle, Lyle, Crocodile*

Record a word that:
- ends in *-ing* (pages 6–7: *living, helping*)
- ends in *-ed* (page 9: *wanted, frightened*)
- ends in *-st* (page 10: *burst, fist*)
- ends in silent *e* (page 11: *take*)
- ends in *-ly* (page 13: *terribly*)
- ends in *-est* (page 14: *nearest*)
- needs a capital letter (page 3: *Mr.* and *Mrs. Primm, Joshua, Lyle*)
- has 3 syllables (page 5: *crocodile*)
- has the prefix *un-* (page 8: *unhappy*)
- has the short *i* sound (page 12: *skip*)

The Great Gracie Chase: Stop That Dog
by Cynthia Rylant

LEARNING ABOUT **Long Vowels**

. . . Gracie loved a quiet house. She loved the kitty sleeping on the windowsill, the big dog sleeping on the couch, the quiet fish going ploop-ploop. For Gracie, a quiet home was the best home.

Gracie Rose was good every single day of her life—except for one . . . the day the painters came.

— From *The Great Gracie Chase*, page 5

On the day the painters came, Gracie "barked and barked and barked and told them to go outside." Gracie was put outside instead, and even though she knew she wasn't supposed to go through the gate by herself, she did.

Everyone in the neighborhood—the painters, the garbage man, the paperboy, and the delivery woman—chased after the run-away Gracie. Soon the whole town was watching or running in the Great Gracie Chase. The bold paintings by Mark Teague complement the lively text describing Gracie's chase to make this a must-have for read-aloud. Share this story to find out how silly little Gracie gets home to her quiet house again.

For practical word-skill practice, reread the story to find out how many long *a* words Cynthia Rylant uses to tell the story of *The Great Gracie Chase*. Have students make STOP signs like the one shown by cutting a circle out of red construction paper, writing STOP on the front, and taping to a tongue depressor. As you reread the story, have students hold up their stop signs every time they hear a long *a* word like *Gracie* and *chase*! Chart the words, and classify them by silent *e*, two vowels walking together, or other long *a* sounds as in *great*.

Stop for Long A

silent e	2 vowels walking together	other long a sounds
named came gate chase take made	painters paint chairs straight air painter great (first vowel does the walking, not the talking)	Gracie say paperboy neighbors sanitation great halfway

For more long vowel practice, have students listen for words with long *e*, *i*, and *o* sounds in the story.

Fritz and the Mess Fairy

by Rosemary Wells

 **LEARNING ABOUT**   Adjectives

"Have you cleaned up your room yet, Fritz?" asked Fritz's mother.

"I will!" shouted Fritz.

Fritz stuffed a month's laundry, twelve heaps of old Halloween candy, half a dozen wet towels, six silver ice cream spoons stuck to six dessert plates, three library books with Popsicle stick bookmarks, and a peanut butter and jelly sandwich all under his bed . . .

— From *Fritz and the Mess Fairy*, pages 4–5

When Fritz's science experiment goes haywire, he meets the messiest of visitors, the Mess Fairy. The meeting inspires Fritz, who is a master-mess-maker himself, to come clean. Will his parents meet the new Fritz in the morning? Parents, teachers, and children alike appreciate the humor and wisdom Rosemary Wells brings to this must-have book.

Demonstrate the power of adjectives with a sentence describing what lies under Fritz's bed. First discuss which of the following ideas sounds more exciting:

laundry	or	*a month's laundry*
candy	or	*twelve heaps of old Halloween candy*
towels	or	*half a dozen wet towels*
spoons	or	*six silver ice cream spoons stuck to six dessert plates*
books	or	*three library books with Popsicle stick bookmarks*
sandwich	or	*a peanut butter and jelly sandwich*

Students unanimously agree that the extra effort of adding few words paints a more vivid picture. Next display the picture on page 5. Ask students to take turns listing items found in the heap at the foot of Fritz's bed. Add adjectives to practice painting pictures with words. Here are a few of our favorite descriptions of Fritz's mess:

bat	to	*old cracked baseball bat*
baseball	to	*muddy baseball*
top	to	*red-and-blue striped top*
cans	to	*four empty soda cans*
ball	to	*deflated soccer ball*
elephant	to	*stuffed elephant with a ripped tail*
books	to	*three overdue library books*

MORE FUN WITH THE BOOK

Get extra mileage from *Fritz and the Mess Fairy* with purposeful rereadings and follow-up spelling activities. Explore synonyms for *said* and phonetic spelling by listing the different words Rosemary Wells uses when a character is talking: *asked, shouted, yelled, grumbled, intoned, squealed, sang, answered, whispered,* and *murmured* are great words for second graders to commit to memory as replacements for the overused *said.*

Even More Must-Have Books for Word Study and Spelling Practice

Me First by Helen Lester

Shy Charles by Rosemary Wells

Daisy Comes Home by Jan Brett

Comet's Nine Lives by Jan Brett

Lyle Finds His Mother by Bernard Waber

The House on East 88th Street by Bernard Waber

Loveable Lyle by Bernard Waber

Lyle and the Birthday Party by Bernard Waber

Name _____ Date _____

_____'s Way

Hello, my name is _____.

I like _____ and _____ and _____.

I always _____.

I never _____.

For breakfast, I always have _____.

I always carry with me _____.

Just in case.

I love to go _____.

In spring, I _____.

In winter, I _____.

In fall, I _____.

And in summer, I _____.

I definitely have my own way of doing things!

Use with *Chester's Way* by Kevin Henkes. • *Teaching With Favorite Read-Alouds in Second Grade*

Chapter 2: Read Along With Me!

10 Must-Have Books for Reading Aloud and Reading Alone

Chapter Learning Goals:
* making simple inferences regarding the order of events
* making predictions about possible outcomes of a story
* using self-correction strategies when reading
* using structural, meaning, and picture clues to determine what makes sense in a story
* relating stories to personal experiences
* identifying the setting, main events, main characters, sequence, and problems in stories
* spelling level-appropriate words using spelling patterns
* reading familiar stories, poems, and passages with fluency and expression

Time for reading aloud and reading alone should be a part of every day of second grade. Allowing time for beginning readers to put newfound skills to the test during independent reading time is vital. Equally important to beginning readers is the motivation that read-aloud time provides.

Get students reading along and counting syllables with Jack Prelutsky's *It's Raining Pigs and Noodles*. Toes will be a-tappin' and students a-readin' with expression in a choral rereading of *Barn Dance!* Identify main characters, setting, and sequence the order of events with *'Twas the Night Before Thanksgiving*. Reinforce fluency during a role-play of *Hey! Get Off Our Train*. Demonstrate the use of reading clues to decode words with *Henry and Mudge Take the Big Test*. Let *Frog and Toad Together* provide more practice in ordering events.

Then *Giggle, Giggle, Quack* with Duck and his barnyard friends. Use *Dragon Gets By* to model how to self-correct reading miscues. Relate to the experiences of the kids in room 207, and then practice using "terrible kid" and "Viola Swamp" voices for a read-along of *Miss Nelson Is Missing!*. Find "loud-mouth" and "frustrated" voices for a performance of *Pigs in the Mud in the Middle of the Rud*.

The ten must-have read-alouds featured in this chapter will have second graders begging to read along and then read alone.

10 Must-Have Books for Reading Aloud and Reading Alone

It's Raining Pigs and Noodles by Jack Prelutsky

Barn Dance! by Bill Martin Jr. and John Archambault

'Twas the Night Before Thanksgiving by Dav Pilkey

Hey! Get Off Our Train by John Burningham

Henry and Mudge Take the Big Test by Cynthia Rylant

Frog and Toad Together by Arnold Lobel

Giggle, Giggle, Quack by Doreen Cronin

Dragon Gets By by Dav Pilkey

Miss Nelson Is Missing! by Harry Allard

Pigs in the Mud in the Middle of the Rud by Lynn Plourde

It's Raining Pigs and Noodles
by Jack Prelutsky

LEARNING ABOUT Syllables and Rhyming Words

It's silent reading time in my second-grade classroom. You could hear a pin drop as I reach for the three favorite Jack Prelutsky books that I keep on my desk. Glancing at the class list inside the front cover of each, I identify the lucky winners: "Sydney, it's your turn to read *The New Kid on the Block*. Michael, you may read *A Pizza the Size of the Sun*, and Allison, you may have *Something BIG Has Been Here*." These three students quickly rush to my desk for the coveted books.

Following our read-aloud of selected Jack Prelutsky poems, I would watch students race to the silent reading library each day in a mad stampede for these books. Introducing sign-up sheets and keeping the books on my desk became a necessity for safety reasons as well as ensuring that everyone had equal time with Jack Prelutsky's rhyming, zany, kid-friendly books.

It's Raining Pigs and Noodles, one of the latest book from the Jack Prelutsky-James Stevenson duo, has created a similar stir in my classroom. With poems like "The Chicken Club," "The Bunny Bus," "My Parents Have the Flu Today," "The Yaks Convened a Meeting," "Never Poke Your Uncle with a Fork," "Winding Through a Maze," "Burp," and "I'm Standing in the Corner," it's no wonder children go wild over these books. From a teacher's perspective, there's no better way to get kids reading with expression and fluency than to give them opportunities to read these poems independently. Whether they're beginning or avid readers, all students pore over the nonsensical lyrics when placed one-on-one with *It's Raining Pigs and Noodles*; they're motivated to read the book for themselves.

Prior to our read-aloud, I chart the title poem, deleting some words and adding some beginning letter clues. I also make a copy for each student. Then we explore syllables, rhyming words, fluency, and expression.

Rich Vocabulary

assorted *adj.*
different kinds

Mrs. L.:	What is it about Jack Prelutsky's poems that makes us want to read them again and again?
Annie:	The silly words.
Kristen:	The rhymes.
Abby:	The beat.
Chris:	The funny pictures
Mrs. L.:	The first time I read this book, I'd read a poem and say to myself, "This is my favorite!" Then I'd read the next page and think, "No, wait, this is my favorite." Then I realized that I liked every poem on every page! To give you a taste of these fun poems, I've charted the title poem, "It's Raining Pigs and Noodles." *(I read the first part of the poem saying "blank" for the missing words.)*

> It's raining pigs and noodles,
> it's pouring frogs and hats,
> chrysanthemums and p(blank),
> bananas, brooms, and c(blank).
> Assorted prunes and parrots
> are dropping from the (blank),
> here comes a bunch of (blank),
> some hippopotami.

Timothy:	Some words are missing.
Mrs. L.:	You're right. Once we identify the pattern of the poem, we can fill in the missing words. Jack Prelutsky is a master at making words fit a pattern. He uses syllables to create the pattern. Read the first two lines with me.
Class:	"It's raining pigs and noodles, it's pouring frogs and hats."
Mrs. L.:	Now read the first line again. Count the syllables on your fingers with me as I write the number of beats below each word:
Class:	"It's rain-ing pigs and nood-les,"
	1 2 3 4 5 6 7
Jenny:	It has seven beats.
Mrs. L.:	I'll write a seven for seven syllables next to this line of the poem. Count the syllables on your fingers as you read line two.
Class:	"It's pouring frogs and hats."
George:	I counted seven beats again.
Dean:	No, six.
Mrs. L.:	Let's count it together. Put a finger up for each beat: "It's"—
Class:	One.
Mrs. L.:	"pour-ing"—
Class:	Two-three.
Mrs. L.:	"frogs and hats"—
Class:	Four, five, six.
Joel:	That's six!
Mrs. L.:	The pattern so far is seven beats, six beats. Let's try to fill in the next line to make a total of seven beats. The first word in line three is tricky.

Teaching With Favorite Read-Alouds in Second Grade

Maggie:	I remember it—*chrysanthemum*.
Mrs. L.:	Excellent remember! There is more than one so it's actually—
Class:	*Chrysanthemums*.
Mrs. L.:	Let's use lines to divide *chrysanthemums* into chunks to see how many syllables it has. Say it slowly. What is the first beat?
Chris:	*Cr*.
Matthew:	You should put the *y* with the first part.
Luke:	The next part is *san*.
Mrs. L.:	Great. *Chry-san*—
David:	*the*
Jesse:	Then *mums*. Wow! That's a four-beat word!
Jake:	*And* makes five beats, so we need a two-beat word.
Hannah:	And it has to start with *p*.
Mrs. L.:	Is there anything else you can tell me about this word?
George:	I bet it rhymes with *hats*.
Sydney:	No, *pats* can't fall like rain. It rhymes with either *noodles* or *pigs*.
Amanda:	*Pigs* isn't at the end of the line. I bet the word rhymes with *noodles*.
Mrs. L.:	So we need a two-beat word that starts with *p* and rhymes with *noodles*.
Jenny:	*Poodles*! *Chrysanthemums* and *poodles*—
Jan:	That makes seven beats for this line.
Mrs. L.:	Great! Keep reading.
Class:	"Bananas, brooms, and"—
Kristen:	*Cats*! You need a *c* word that rhymes with *hats*. That's *cats* because cats are falling like rain, too.
Mrs. L.:	Let's count the syllables in this line to see if it fits the pattern. We'll draw lines on bananas to show the syllables.
David:	*Ba-nan-as*.
Maggie:	It's a three-beat word.
Joel:	*Brooms* and *cats* makes three more beats: three plus three makes six beats.
Mrs. L.:	Excellent! Jack Prelutsky did make a seven-six-seven-six pattern. The rhythm of these syllables make it fun to read the poem out loud. Let's read the first four lines all together.
Class:	"It's raining pigs and noodles, it's pouring frogs and hats, chrysanthemums and poodles, bananas, brooms, and cats."
Mrs. L.:	Let's find out if the next four lines follow the pattern.
	Assorted prunes and parrots
	are dropping from the (blank),
	here comes a bunch of (blank),
	some hippopotami.
Kristen:	I think the prunes and parrots are dropping from the sky.
Mrs. L.:	There's no beginning letter clue for this line. But it does make sense that these things would fall from the sky.
Kristen:	It has to be *sky*.

Mrs. L.:	Let's count the syllables in these next two lines. Put up a finger as I read, please: "As-sort-ed prunes and par-rots"—
Class:	Seven beats!
Mrs. L.:	"Are drop-ping from the sky."
Class:	Six beats!
Timothy:	It follows the pattern!
Mrs. L.:	"Here comes a bunch of (blank)." What do you know about this missing word?
Matthew:	It starts with *c*.
Chris:	"Here comes a bunch" has four beats.
Luke:	*Of* is a one-beat word. That makes five beats. So it has to be a two-beat word that starts with *c*. That will make seven beats in that line.
Amanda:	And it has to rhyme with *parrots*.
Michael:	It's *carrots*.
Mrs. L.:	"Here comes a bunch of carrots." Carrots do come in bunches. I think you're right! How many beats does the line have?
Class:	One, two, three, four, five, six-seven.
Allison:	That's seven beats!
Mrs. L.:	Look at the long word at the end of the next line. Let's break it apart by sylla-bles: *hip-po-pot-a-mi (I stress the syllables as I say the word)*.
Hannah:	*Hip*.
Timothy:	*Po*.
Luke:	*Pot*.
Jesse:	*A*.
Michael:	*Mi*! Doesn't he mean *hippopotamus*?
Mrs. L.:	More than one hippopotamus is falling from the sky. Jack Prelutsky couldn't write *hippopotamuses*. Can you tell me why?
Kristen:	It's too hard to say.
Mrs. L.:	I agree. And, it's also adds too many syllables to that line. He used a play on words and made it *hip-po-pot-a-mi*, which is a fancy way to mean more than one when you're talking about animals. Octopuses are sometimes called octopi, for example. How many syllables does *hip-po-pot-a-mi* have?
Class:	Five!
Mrs. L.:	So "some hippopotami" would have—
Class:	Six beats!
Mrs. L.:	Excellent! Let's put the first part of this poem back together. Read the lines with expression.

Then students work with partners to fill in the missing words and draw lines to mark syllables on their copies of the poem. Our chart is displayed for assistance with the first part of the poem. The second verse also has deleted words. Note that only one of the four pairs of lines in it follows the rhyming word spelling pattern of the first verse.; for example, *Train* and *rain* do look and sound alike, but *nickels* and *pickles* only sound alike.

Following this independent work time, hold a discussion of look-alike and sound-alike rhyming word pairs as partners share their responses.

MORE FUN WITH THE BOOK

Share all the hilarious kid-approved poems from *It's Raining Pigs and Noodles* for read-aloud. Reread favorites to kick off silent reading time. Make a tally table of those deemed favorites by your students for even more book-based skill learning.

OUR FAVORITE JACK PRELUTSKY BOOK	
Something BIG Has Been Here	ℍℍℍ ℍℍℍ
The New Kid on the Block	ℍℍℍ
A Pizza the Size of the Sun	//
It's Raining Pigs and Noodles	ℍℍℍ ℍℍℍ

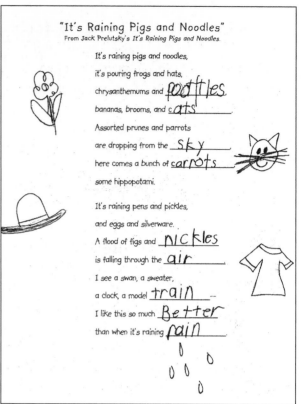

Classroom sample

Pocket Chart Center

TEACHING TIP

Organize materials near a pocket chart to create an Independent learning center where students can do sequencing activities, practice sight words, sort words by attribute, and more! Write the related book titles on the front of individual 10 x 13 manila envelopes. Laminate each envelope, making sure the flap is open and the clasp is pressed flat. Use an Exacto knife to slit the opening of the envelope, slip inside a copy of the book, sentence strips, and any recording sheets. Place the envelopes in a box or tub near the pocket chart. Introduce the activities, and then invite students to choose activities to explore during free time. Our center for *It's Raining Pigs and Noodles* is shown at left.

More Must-Have Books for Reading Aloud and Reading Alone

Barn Dance!
by Bill Martin Jr. and John Archambault

LEARNING ABOUT Reading Fluently

A few pages into *Barn Dance!*, you're guaranteed to see toes a-tappin' as you read aloud this rollicking story. On a full-moon night, one special boy is privy to what happens in the barn while the rest of the family sleeps. Second graders fall under a spell as they listen to the sing-song verse and want to hear it over and over again. *Barn Dance!* fans are impressed by the young boy's determination to satisfy his growing curiosity by venturing to the barn at night. Readers are equally thrilled when the kid "danced his little toe through a hole in his stockin'!" When the night owl warned that "mornin's comin' closer," the boy slipped past the "ol' dog in just the nick of time, an' tiptoed up the stairs as quiet as a feather on a breath of air. He hummed a little do-si-do an' flopped himself in bed. With the wonder of the barn dance . . . dancin' in his head." As students listen, many will be committing the beat of the book to heart, anxious to read along, to try out the flow of the words.

Gather students for a choral reading that is sure to inspire reading with fluency and expression. Prior to reading it aloud, read the book independently to rehearse the beat that Bill Martin Jr. and John Archambault build with skillfully crafted text. With the beat in mind, invite students to be your echo and mimic a line-by-line rereading of the book.

> **Rich Vocabulary**
>
> **wonderment** *n.* when you feel greatly surprised

Mrs. L.:	"Full moon shinin', shinin' big an' bright,"
Class:	"Full moon shinin', shinin' big an' bright,"
Mrs. L.:	"Pushin' back the shadows, holdin' back the night."
Class:	"Pushin' back the shadows, holdin' back the night."
Mrs. L.:	"Not a thing stirrin', quiet as could be,"
Class:	"Not a thing stirrin', quiet as could be,"
Mrs. L.:	"Just the whisper of the leaves on the cottonwood tree."
Class:	"Just the whisper of the leaves on the cottonwood tree."

'Twas the Night Before Thanksgiving
by Dav Pilkey

LEARNING ABOUT Reading Fluency

'Twas the day before Thanksgiving
And all through the trees,
The fall leaves were spinning
Aloft in the breeze.
Eight children had boarded
Their school bus with grins
In hopes that a field trip
Soon would begin.

— From *'Twas the Night Before Thanksgiving,* pages 4–5

The predictable beat and rhyming words make Dav Pilkey's comical take on the 'twas the night before theme a hit with second graders. On a field trip to a turkey farm on the day before Thanksgiving, the children spot Farmer Mack Nuggett's ax propped by the door. Putting two and two together, the children end up confiscating the turkeys who ultimately end up at Thanksgiving dinner—as guests, of course. Share this great book the day before Thanksgiving vacation, and you may encourage a few Thanksgiving Day vegetarians as students sympathize with the turkeys' plight.

Chances are you will be asked to read this rhyming tale over and over. As you reread, students may chime in the rhyming word pairs from memory. Take time to identify the modern-day farm setting of the field trip and the main characters—Farmer Mack Nuggett, the children, their teacher; and the eight turkeys named Ollie, Stanley, Larry, Moe, Wally, Beaver, Shemp and Groucho are memorable, for sure!

Provide sentence strips from the poem for students to place in order on a pocket chart for retelling and rereading with fluency. Invite groups to illustrate different scenes from the story, and have them place their pictures in sequential order on a pocket chart and then match them to the corresponding sentence strips. As students rehearse the poem over and over again, reading fluency and spelling are reinforced with each rereading.

Rich Vocabulary

embraces *v.* hugs

grim *adj.* horrible

MORE FUN WITH THE BOOK
For added entertainment and extension, challenge students to invent their own rhyming lines for a selected part of the story.

When what with their wondering eyes should they see,
But a dancing white stallion
And a little turkey.

Hey! Get Off Our Train

by John Burningham

LEARNING ABOUT ## Reading With Expression

As a boy drifts off to sleep with his "pajama case dog" tucked in the crook of his arm, miniature versions of the same boy and dog matter-of-factly prepare for a train ride. John Burningham's dark and misty illustrations enhance the dreamlike quality of the story.

Each time the boy and his dog get off the train to have a picnic, play ghosts, go for a swim, or throw snowballs, a new animal climbs aboard. "Hey! Get off our train," the boy and his dog chant together. "Please let me come with you on your train," each animal begs and then pleads its case to stay. In the end, an elephant, seal, crane, tiger, and polar bear are riding on the train to avoid individual environmental atrocities such as polluted water, fur trading, and disappearing wetlands. Young readers, like the boy in the story, sympathize with the animals who need better places to live.

Just when readers are convinced the boy is having a dream, they are taken back to his room where he is just waking up. His mother stands over him saying, "Get up immediately. . . . There are lots of animals in the house. There's an elephant in the hall, a seal in the bathtub, a crane in the laundry, a tiger on the stairs, and a polar bear by the fridge. Does this have anything to do with you?"

Reread the story, and have some role-playing fun while reinforcing reading with expression, word recognition, and fluency. Prior to the read-aloud, copy repetitive lines and animal speeches onto sentence strips, such as the following:

> **All:** "Hey! Get off our train!"
> **Elephant:** "Please let me come with you on your train. Someone is coming to cut off my tusks, and soon there will be none of us left."

As you reread the story, call on volunteers to read the parts of individual animals. Invite the rest of the students to chime in on the repetitive sentences, "Hey! Get off our train," "Please let me come with you on your train," and "soon there will be none of us left." Ask each volunteer to plead his or her animal's case to join the train ride. Remind speakers to use expressive voices to convince the audience and win a seat on the train. Read the story again and again with different volunteers reading the lines for each animal. Take the show on the road, and perform for other classes to spread the word about protecting endangered animals.

Rich Vocabulary

plight n. a difficult situation

Henry and Mudge Take the Big Test
by Cynthia Rylant

LEARNING ABOUT Word Recognition

Mudge was not a perfect student.
He liked to lay down too much.
He liked to sniff the other students.
He liked to think about other things.
But he always showed up.
And he always wagged his tail.
And he always gave his teacher a kiss.

— From *Henry and Mudge Take the Big Test*, pages 29–30

In this tenth book of their adventures, Henry and Mudge meet a smart dog, go to dog school, and take a big test. Cynthia Rylant knows just what it takes to grab second graders' attention and does so with words perfect for newly independent readers. Read aloud *Henry and Mudge Take the Big Test* to motivate your students for independent book-browsing time.

Although the book is geared more for independent reading than read-aloud, its repetitive text and limited vocabulary provides ample opportunity for demonstrating voice inflection and expression when reading. Susie Stevenson's cartoon-style drawings give picture clues for decoding words like *drool, liver treats, collar, certificate,* and *nervous*. Scan the text for these and other words for students to decode prior to the read-aloud.

Introduce a mini-lesson that shows the variety of ways to figure out unknown words when reading independently. Stress that good readers think about what makes sense while using all the available clues—picture, structural, and context or meaning clues. Chart sentences from the story, deleting words and providing multiple-choice answers. Together, read the options, discuss which word fits the clues, and then figure out the unknown word. Put the sentences back together to practice fluency and to demonstrate self-correction techniques. Check out my class's thought processes in the example below.

A man with a c_____ walked by.
   A. hat
   B. can
   C. collie
   D. book

Letter clues: *The unknown word begins with* c.
Picture clues: *The man has a hat and is walking a dog on a leash.*

Rich Vocabulary

mind *v.* to do what is asked

Meaning clues: The c word must be a "dog" word.
Solution: This means the answer must be collie. The picture looks like a collie. (Chris has a dog that looks like this, and it's a miniature collie).

More Henry and Mudge Books

More Henry and Mudge Books

Henry and Mudge-The First Book of Their Adventures
Henry and Mudge in Puddle Trouble
Henry and Mudge in the Green Time
Henry and Mudge Under the Yellow Moon
Henry and Mudge in the Sparkle Days
Henry and Mudge and the Bedtime Thumps

Frog and Toad Together
by Arnold Lobel

LEARNING ABOUT **Making Inferences And Sequencing**

When Frog and Toad get together, there's usually a sequence of humorous events leading to a self-created calamity. In this collection of five stories, Frog and Toad tackle a list of things to do, wait for the garden to grow, rustle up some will power, put their bravery to the test, and are thankful dreams don't always come true.

Author Arnold Lobel has created books that children can't wait to get their hands on. The vocabulary and amount of text per page make these tales perfect for independent reading by second graders. The adventures featuring this comical, worrisome, and a bit over-reactive pair make great read-alouds as well; the subtle humor of both text and illustrations afford children and adults a pleasurable book-sharing time.

Read aloud *Frog and Toad Together*, and then use the activities below to get students making inferences about the order of events and possible outcomes of each story.

After reading "A List," display sentence strips of each item on Toad's list in scrambled order. Have individuals place the events in proper order, while the rest of the class numbers the corresponding event on a copy of the reproducible on page 41. Second graders are quick to point out that it's easier to play games with Frog if you go to his house first—and it's best to wake up prior to taking a walk! Then let students order the main events in "The Garden." Have them list the main events for one of the other stories in the book on the back of the reproducible. Meet together to share their main-events lists.

Rich Vocabulary

wailed *v.* cried loudly

Giggle, Giggle, Quack
by Doreen Cronin

Retelling A Story

Farmer Brown leaves his brother, Bob, in charge of the animals while he takes a much-needed vacation. The farmer's parting words are, "Keep an eye on Duck. He's trouble." But Bob turns his back on Duck to wave good-bye, so he doesn't see that Duck has spotted a pencil on the ground.

Would Farmer Brown really have pizza delivered to the animals, let the pigs take baths with his favorite bubble bath and good towels, and allow the cows to pick a movie for movie night? Did Duck and the pencil have something to do with the notes giving permission for these treats?

Second graders will enjoy the knee-slapping humor of *Giggle, Giggle, Quack*, the follow-up to what's happening in the barnyard after *Click, Clack, Moo: Cows That Type*. Invite students to join in on the giggles, quacks, moos, and oinks during repeated rereadings of this must-have book.

Then divide the class into groups of pigs, ducks, hens, and cows. Set each group to task with paper, pencils, and a designated Duck to be the recorder. Ask each group to compose one to two sentences retelling its animal's part of the story. Next gather the class together. Act as the narrator, and segue from one group to another to tell the story. After each note is shared, let everyone chime in with the appropriate giggle, giggle, cluck, oink, moo, or quack. This is a sample from my classroom.

Narrator: Farmer Brown needed a vacation. So he called on his brother, Bob, to lend a hand with the animals. "Keep an eye on that duck because he's trouble," Farmer Brown warned as he drove off. Duck finds a pencil while Bob is waving to his brother. The hens tell Duck what to write.
Hens: We like to have pizza on Tuesday night. Real, not frozen. The hens like anchovies.
Everyone: Giggle, giggle, cluck.

Rich Vocabulary

sensitive *adj.* to have your feelings easily hurt

influence *v.* to have an effect on

The story ends when Farmer Brown calls to check on things, and Duck answers the phone. The only thing Farmer Brown hears is "Giggle, giggle, quack, giggle, moo, giggle, oink . . ." Uh-oh! Students will ask for more and more rereadings of the story of Duck and his farmyard friends.

Dragon Gets By

by Dav Pilkey

LEARNING ABOUT
Self-Correcting Reading Strategies

We all have those days. The alarm doesn't go off, we can't find the car keys, there's an empty carton of milk in the fridge, and the dog has chewed our favorite shoe. Dragon is having one of those days. He reads an egg, fries his newspaper, and dusts his dirt floor until it becomes a basement. Things don't improve much for Dragon during the day, but he does get by.

Readers accompany Dragon through five stories about his mixed-up day. Children will giggle at the comical illustrations as Dragon "butters his tea and sips a cup of toast" in "Dragon Sees the Day." Read aloud this first story, and relate Dragon's bad day to similar ones of your own. Ask students about their own bad days. Let Dragon's story provide inspiration for writers' workshop stories based on these experiences.

Then read aloud the opening page of "Housework" where Dragon sweeps his living room floor with a lawnmower. Take his lead, and make a few miscues by substituting incorrect words such as the following:

Dragon's floor was very delicious.

He got his cat and began to sweep.

Continue making similar miscues until someone stops you. Or stop and say, "That doesn't make sense. I'd better reread that sentence." After modeling self-correction with a few more examples, discuss how good readers stop after each page or so to think about what is happening in the story, to ensure that the story makes sense, and to reread those parts that do not.

For more practice, read the remaining stories in *Dragon Gets By*. Chart sentences from the book for more miscue practice. The illustrations with the sentences below provide picture clues to help with corrections.

1. *All of his sweeping left a very big hat on his floor.* (page 15)
2. *"What's gong on in hair?" asked the mailmouse.* (page 17)
3. *Dragon looked at the big pile of dogs in his yard.* (page 20)
4. *Dragon looked in his refrigerator, but there was no food at all.* (page 26)
5. *It had been a long, busy day, and now it was breakfast.* (page 46)

***Answers:** 1. hat should be hole 2. hair should be here 3. dogs should be dirt 4. refrigerator should be cupboard 5. breakfast should be bedtime*

Rich Vocabulary

groggy *adj.* not thinking clearly, often from being sleepy

Miss Nelson Is Missing!
by Henry Allard

LEARNING ABOUT **Punctuation and Reading Expressively**

The kids in Room 207 were misbehaving again.
Spitballs stuck to the ceiling.
Paper planes whizzed through the air.
They were the worst-behaved class in the whole school.
"Now settle down," said Miss Nelson in a sweet voice.

— From *Miss Nelson Is Missing!*, page 3

But the whispering, giggling, squirming, and rudeness continue—until the next day. Miss Nelson is missing, and Viola Swamp is the substitute. The kids just know she's a real witch; her ugly black dress and hissing voice don't fool them. After days and days of working harder than ever, there's still no sign of Miss Nelson anywhere. How much more of Viola Swamp will Room 207 have to endure? Have Miss Nelson's kids learned their lesson? Does Miss Nelson have a secret?

Share this book for read-aloud when your students are in a misbehaving mood. Compare James Marshall's picture of Miss Nelson's class on page 9 with the one of Miss Swamp's class on page 29. Or take a cue from Miss Nelson, and show up the next day wearing a black dress and striped stockings and greet your students in a hissing Viola Swamp voice!

The italicized words, descriptive text, and dialogue in this book are perfect for a motivating lesson on reading with expression. Display the book to show how Harry Allard and James Marshall worked together to combine words and pictures that accurately portray the feelings and emotions of the characters. Introduce the lesson by using the text on page 8 and the picture on page 9.

"Wow!" yelled the kids. "Now we can really act up!"
"Today let's be just terrible!" they said.

Ask students to read the words in their most terrible kids' voices. Answer them with your most hissing Viola Swamp voice: "Not so fast!"

Chart sentences from the story for students to read with expression. Discuss the use of italicized words, exclamation marks, and quotation marks as hints for expression. Talk about how good readers glance ahead to see who is talking so they can adjust their voice accordingly when it's their turn to read. Have extra copies of *Miss Nelson Is Missing!* on hand for silent reading but be prepared to hear some hissing and sweet teacher voices as students read this must-have book independently.

Rich Vocabulary

discouraged *adj.*
without hope

Pigs in the Mud in the Middle of the Rud

by Lynn Plourde

LEARNING ABOUT Reading Expressively

It had rained. It had poured.
Now a Model T Ford
was stopped in the rud
by some pigs in the mud.

— From *Pigs in the Mud in the Middle of the Rud,* page 4

First it's pigs, then it's hens, sheep, and bulls keeping the family from getting through. One by one, Brother, Sister, Mama, and Papa do their best to shoo the animals out of the way without success, but Grandma's dander's up. With the words "TIME FOR SUP!" she clears the road. The comical ending finds Grandma covered from head to toe with the mud in the middle of the rud, thanks to the stampeding animals.

Lynn Plourde combines rhyming word pairs and nonsense words like *shmuffle, smatter,* and *smarge* with a beat that gets children participating from the very first page. The inspiration for this book came to the author when she looked out her window and saw eight piglets running down the middle of the rud (a *rud* is a road if you live in Maine). It's no surprise that Plourde is also a speech and language therapist and the author of ten books on listening and speaking.

Second graders love listening to and speaking the parts of the characters having trouble with the pigs. As an added bonus, each sentence spoken by Grandma is printed in bold red letters. The illustrations by Caldecott Medal winner, John Schoenherr *(Owl Moon)*, give humor to this book; the animals' expressions and interactions with each other and the family members give readers much to pore over.

Share this story for read-aloud. Then read it again, inviting children to read along. Point to the words as you read, stress rhyming words, and play with reading expressively as each character speaks. Find voices for Grandma, the narrator, and the other characters. Try out the repeated phrases shown below.

"Oh, no. Won't do. Gotta shoo. But who?" (frustrated narrator's voice)

"I'll shoo. That's who." (different voice for each character)

Grandma's Loudly-Mouthed Words:

"Pigs in the rud!"

"Hens in the rud!"

"Sheep in the rud!"

"Bulls in the rud!"

"OOOOOO-EEE!"

"TIME FOR SUP!"

Rich Vocabulary

snarl *v.* to speak in a grumpy voice

During silent reading, have small groups of students pair up to read aloud the story using different character voices. Tell each group to designate a narrator, Brother, Sister, Mama, Papa, and Grandma. They may perform their versions of the story for classmates following silent reading time.

A performance of *Pigs in the Mud in the Middle of the Rud*

Even More Must-Have Books for Reading Along and Reading Alone

Falling Up by Shel Silverstein

Where the Sidewalk Ends by Shel Silverstein

The New Kid on the Block by Jack Prelutsky

A Pizza the Size of the Sun by Jack Prelutsky

Mr. Putter and Tabby Pour the Tea by Cynthia Rylant

Poppleton Forever by Cynthia Rylant

What's First on the List?

Directions: Number the items on Toad's list from 1 to 10.

A List of Things To Do Today
___ Play games with Frog
___ Go to Frog's house
___ Go to sleep
___ Get dressed
___ Take walk with Frog
___ Wake up
___ Take nap
___ Eat supper
___ Eat lunch
___ Eat breakfast

Number the main events in the story of "The Garden."
Write 1 beside the first thing that happened.

_____ The seeds are still afraid to grow.

_____ Toad plants the flower seeds.

_____ At last, the seeds stop being afraid to grow.

_____ Frog gives Toad some flower seeds.

_____ Toad sings song songs, reads poems, and plays music for his seeds.

_____ The seeds are afraid to grow.

BONUS: On the back of this sheet, list the main events in "Cookies," "Dragons and Giants," or "The Dream."

Use with *Frog and Toad Together.* • *Teaching With Favorite Read-Alouds in Second Grade*

Chapter 3: What Do You Think?
10 Must-Have Thought-Provoking Books to Spark Writing

Chapter Learning Goals:

* using prewriting strategies to plan written work
* using strategies to draft and revise written work
* evaluating one's own and others' writing
* using strategies to organize written work
* using writing and other methods to describe familiar experiences
* using descriptive words and adjectives to convey basic ideas
* writing in a variety of forms and genres
* reading aloud and talking about thought-provoking books

What is it about certain books and authors that makes even the youngest readers gravitate to them? Sometimes these books put into words our own memories of similar experiences. Sometimes we laugh at or cry with the characters. Some books offer us perspectives we wouldn't have thought of on our own. Others open our eyes to situations we never knew existed. Thought-provoking books stir something inside readers and allow them to express what otherwise may have gone unexpressed.

The books in this chapter offer a sampling of different tones, voices, and writing styles. Share these thought-provoking books for read-aloud, and then open up discussions that lead your beginning writers to put pencils to paper to meet a variety of goals. Learn prewriting strategies to plan a letter to Eric Carle after reading *"Slowly, Slowly, Slowly," Said the Sloth*. Use *If You Were a Writer* to work with students before they write a what-if story. Write your personal memoir with inspiration from *My Rotten Redheaded Older Brother*, and then help young writers evaluate their own and others' writing. Have students write informational pieces based on *All the Places to Love* and *Sophie Skates*.

---

10 Must-Have Thought-Provoking Books to Spark Writing

"Slowly, Slowly, Slowly," Said the Sloth by Eric Carle

If You Were a Writer by Joan Lowery Nixon

My Rotten Redheaded Older Brother by Patricia Polacco

All the Places to Love by Patricia MacLachlan

Sophie Skates by Rachel Isadora

The Amazing Bone by William Steig

When Jessie Came Across the Sea by Amy Hest

So You Want to Be President by Judith St. George

Berlioz the Bear by Jan Brett

The Wednesday Surprise by Eve Bunting

Explore descriptive language in *The Amazing Bone*, and then add "just a few more words" to a journal entry from *When Jessie Came Across the Sea*. Let students note what it takes to be president as they read *So You Want to Be President* and then write their own campaign announcements. Urge students to write newspaper articles featuring the orchestra perform-ance at the gala ball in *Berlioz the Bear*, and their own memoirs with inspiration from *The Wednesday Surprise*.

Second graders will be talking, writing, and sharing what they think about the inspira-tional books in this chapter.

"Slowly, Slowly, Slowly" Said the Sloth

by Eric Carle

LEARNING ABOUT Writing a Letter

Why are we always in a hurry?
Rush. Rush. Rush.
We scurry from here and there.
We play computer games and then—
quick! click!—we watch TV. We eat fast food.
Everyone tells us to make it snappy!
Hurry up! Time is flying! Step on it!
There's so little time just to be with friends,
to watch a sunset or gaze at a star-filled sky.
Ah, what we could learn—even if just a little—
from the gentle sloth who slowly, slowly, slowly
crawls along a branch of a tree,
eats a little, sleeps a lot,
and lives in peace.

— From *"Slowly, Slowly, Slowly," Said the Sloth*, back cover

Rich Vocabulary

dawdle *v.* to walk in a slow way

mellow *adj.* calm

It is with great insight and respect that Eric Carle writes this story about the lackadaisical, languid, unflappable, lethargic, mellow, laid-back sloth. Ah, what we could learn from this gentle animal. Jane Goodall writes in the forward to this must-have book that when she was a child, " . . . sloths, although they were sometimes hunted for food by the indigenous people, had little else to fear. Today they face the destruction of their habitat as forests are cut down for timber or to create grazing land for cattle."

Like Jane Goodall (and countless others, I'm sure), I am delighted that Eric Carle has written this book about sloths. While any book by Carle is a treat, this book offers hope. By making young children aware of sloths, he is inspiring future generations to care about the animals who depend on us and with whom we share our world. And perhaps the peaceful and tranquil sloth will make a lasting impression on children growing up in our fast-paced, remote-controlled, cellular world; maybe after reading this book, they will make time to watch sunsets and gaze at the star-filled skies with friends.

Kick off a read-aloud and discussion of *"Slowly, Slowly, Slowly," Said the Sloth* with sloth trivia questions based on facts from Jane Goodall's foreword to the book.

1. Some sloths have three toes. Others have two toes. (true)
2. Sloths can turn their heads about 270 degrees. (true)
3. Sloths can rotate their bodies almost 360 degrees (a full circle). (true)
4. Sloths sleep for 15–19 hours out of 24. (true)
5. Sloths are green. (False, but algae grows on their long hairs so that they become the same greenish color as the forest around them.)
6. Sloths sleep upside down with their head resting on their bellies. (true)
7. All kinds of frogs and turtles live in their fur. (False, but moths and beetles do.)
8. Sloths protect themselves with dagger-like claws. (true)
9. Sloths live in the same tree for days, sometimes for weeks, and climb down to go to the bathroom about once a week. (true)
10. Sloths can "talk." (True; they may not talk like we do, but they make a gentle sigh that sounds like "ah-ee.")

The next day take the book back to a writers' workshop mini-lesson for a prewriting activity that will help students organize their thoughts for a letter to author Eric Carle. After students gather clipboards, pencils, and paper, I invite them to "slowly, slowly, slowly" meet me on the carpet for our writers' workshop meeting. Our slow-paced lesson based on the tranquil sloth goes something like this.

Mrs. L.:	I like the slothful way you slowly . . . slowly . . . slowly . . . came to our writers' meeting.
Amanda:	Do we get to read the sloth book again?
Mrs. L.:	We had so much to talk about after reading *"Slowly, Slowly, Slowly," Said the Sloth* yesterday. I thought we should continue our discussion by taking another look at this great book. Then I thought it would be nice if you shared some of your comments with Eric Carle.
Kristen:	The author? Is he coming here?
Mrs. L.:	No, I thought we'd send your ideas to him in a letter.
Dean:	Is that why we need clipboards and pencils?
Mrs. L.:	Yes. As I reread the story, I'd like you to jot down ideas you would like to share with Eric Carle. Maybe, for example, you love the illustration of the armadillo or the porcupine or the sleeping sloth. You might draw a quick pic-

	ture of the porcupine or write the animal word to help you remember this idea when you go to write your letter.
Maggie:	I like how he writes "slowly, slowly, slowly" three times to make us know how slow the sloth is.
Mrs. L.:	You could write *slowly* three times to help you remember this idea.
Allison:	How many ideas should we have?
Mrs. L.:	That's up to you. But, I would think with all the things you had to tell me about this book yesterday, everyone should be able to think of at least three things to write to Mr. Carle. I'll read the book slowly so you can jot down ideas. After each page, look at me and smile to let me know you're ready for me to continue. *(I slowly reread the book in its entirety, pausing for students to record ideas, which we then discuss.)*
David:	I like all the words he wrote on the last page.
Sydney:	I wrote that down, too.
Mrs. L.:	What are you going to tell Eric Carle you like about this page?
Sydney:	At first, I thought the sloth was ignoring the animals because they were calling him lazy and boring and slow and that's not nice.
David:	But he was really thinking about how to answer them. The words on the last page are great because he lets them know he's not lazy.
Mrs. L.:	Let me show you the last two pages of text. Here's something I like. *(I hold up the book to display the last two pages of text.)* See how Eric Carle uses spaces on this page.
Michael:	The spaces make you read it slower.
Mrs. L.:	Yes, if you want to read this book with expression, you must read the sloth's words more slowly. The extra spaces help readers know to read slowly.
Allison:	That's where the sloth tells the other animals that that's just the way he is.
Mrs. L.:	I know that's why I like that part. He's standing up for himself. And he accepts himself for whom he really is—even though he's different.
Jan:	I like the next page that shows all the animals. I wanted to know what some of the animals were so I looked at their names.
Mrs. L.:	This is a helpful research page. I'd never heard of a coati or a peccary or a tapir . . . or a hoatzin.
Michael:	I thought there was an alligator on that page but you read the word *caiman*. I bet it's related to the alligator.
Jenny:	You could ask Eric Carle that in your letter.
Mrs. L.:	Good thinking. What else impressed you about this book?
Hannah:	*(drawing with her finger)* I like the way he made the sloth's eyes like this to show he is sleeping in the dark.
Mrs. L.:	You could draw your own sleeping sloth for Mr. Carle.
Luke:	I'm going to thank him for teaching me about sloths.
Matthew:	I'm going to tell him that he made me want a sloth for a pet.
Mrs. L.:	I'm going to tell him I learned that I shouldn't always be in a hurry—or tell my students and my own children to "rush, rush, rush." On the back of the book,

Teaching With Favorite Read-Alouds in Second Grade

	he reminds us that we should take time to just be with friends, and watch a sunset or look at a star-filled sky. I'm going to try spend time doing something slowly, slowly, slowly, like the sloth.
George:	I like how the sloth puts out his sharp claws at the crocodile.
Mrs. L.:	You mean the caiman? I didn't notice that. Let's take a look.
George:	I remember from the trivia questions you read yesterday that sloths use their fingernails like knives to protect themselves from enemies.
Mrs. L.:	I see what you mean. His dagger-like claw looks ready to strike out. The caiman's teeth are pretty close to him. Good thinking, George.
Luke:	The claws are out again when the jaguar comes nearby.
Mrs. L.:	What excellent observers you are. You have many excellent observations to share with Mr. Carle about his book. I'm sure he'll be impressed. Now it's time to put your ideas into the form of a letter.

Then we talk about the form of a letter. On the board, I model the parts that must be included in every letter.

> *March 28, 2003*
> *Dear Mr. Carle,*
> *Paragraph #1: Introduce yourself, and tell about our read-aloud of his book "Slowly, Slowly, Slowly," Said the Sloth.*
> *Paragraph #2: Tell three things you liked about the book or ask questions you have.*
> *Paragraph #3: Thank Mr. Carle for reading your letter, and invite him to write back.*
> *Sincerely,*
> *Your Name*

I send students to their seats to work on rough drafts and illustrations for their letters. Over the course of the next several writers' workshop periods, I hold individual conferences with writers and help them get their letters into final copy form. When all the letters have been completed, we sign, seal, address, and deliver the envelope to the school office where it will be placed with other outgoing mail.

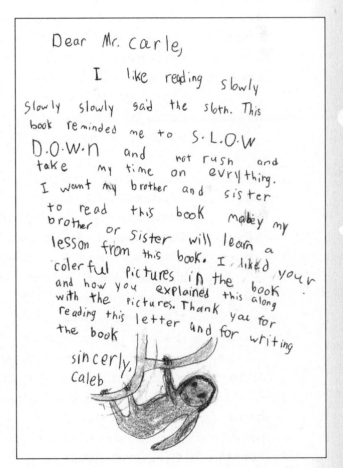

A letter to Eric Carle

How to Contact Eric Carle

Visit Eric Carle at his website **www.eric-carle.com**, or send him "snail mail" to the following address: P.O. Box 485, Northampton, MA 01060

More Must-Have Thought-Provoking Books to Spark Writing

···

If You Were a Writer
by Joan Lowery Nixon

LEARNING ABOUT **The Writing Process**

Melia's mother was a writer. Sometimes she sat at her typewriter and her fingers bounced over the keys. Sometimes she stared at the paper in the typewriter and sat so still that Melia thought she was like a fairy-tale princess who had been turned into stone by an evil spell.

— From *If You Were a Writer*, page 7

If You Were a Writer is a book with a multitude of uses for teaching beginning writers. Kick off a year of book-based writers' workshop mini-lessons with a read-aloud of this book. Second-grade writers will listen attentively as Melia peppers her mother with questions about how a writer knows the right words, finds ideas for writing, starts a story, and turns one idea into a whole story. Melia's mother patiently responds with thoughtful answers that help Melia on her way to becoming a writer, too.

A writers' workshop lesson based on *If You Were a Writer*

Let Melia's question-and-answer session with her mother lay the foundation and provide direction for your writers' workshop. Reread specific pages to focus instruction of skills for a variety of lessons such as thinking of what-ifs, working with words, and inventing exciting story beginnings. After reading aloud the book, adapt the following plan to jumpstart a year of writers' workshop lessons that will have your students under a writers' spell in no time at all.

Rich Vocabulary

murmured *v.* said in a low, quiet voice

dashed *v.* moved quickly

Teaching With Favorite Read-Alouds in Second Grade

Writers' Workshop Plan Based on *If You Were a Writer*

Day 1: Words That Make Pictures

Mother's silky blouse was slippery, slithery, and soft; the apple pie's fragrance was spicy, sweet, and sour. Share a bag of objects, and have children think of describing words for each object.

Day 2: Words That Show

Characters don't just walk; they stomp, stamp, stumble, stagger, tiptoe and trip, tumble and trip, droop and drop, snore and sleep. Write words such as *said* and *eat* on index cards, and place in a hat. Challenge groups of students to think of synonyms that do a better job of describing each action.

Day 3: Ideas Are Everywhere

What if a bear stole the honey? What if a monster from outer space was after a little black dog? Make a list of potential what-if story ideas to display at the writing center for those days when a writer needs help in getting started.

Day 4: Meet the Characters

What is Melia really like? As a class, chart her character traits and provide support from the story for each. Have students revisit a familiar story to add words that describe a particular character.

Day 5: Introduce Story-Sharing Etiquette

Encourage active listening skills in students while you share one of your own stories. Remind them to keep their eyes on the speaker, their ears open, their hands in their laps, and their mouths closed. Then ask for their feedback.

(For more writers' workshop ideas based on *If You Were a Writer,* see *Literature-Based Mini-Lessons to Teach Writing* by Susan Lunsford, Scholastic Professional Books, 1998.)

My Rotten Redheaded Older Brother
by Patricia Polacco

 **LEARNING ABOUT**   ## Writing from Experience

Rich Vocabulary

inspired *v.* to become more happy at the idea of something

Tricia's older brother, Richard, could do everything better than she could—run the fastest, burp the loudest, get the dirtiest, and—he was four years older, as he reminded her often.

So, when Bubbie tells Tricia that wishes made on falling stars always come true, Tricia waits and watches the night sky for the next one and wishes "to do something—anything—better than her big brother." The wish comes true all right—Tricia's something better was to fall off the merry-go-round, pass out, and have to get stitches. Later she confides to Bubbie that her wish had come true differently than she thought it would.

This comical story based on Patricia Polacco's real experiences with her brother, Richard, evokes sympathy from second graders no matter what their rank is in the families. Share *My Rotten Redheaded Older Brother* for read-aloud, and then bring the story to a writers' workshop mini-lesson where students can write down family experiences of their own.

TEACHING TIP

During writing time, I work on my story, *My Rotten Blonde-Haired Older Brother*. This work-in-progress becomes a model for my students as well as a reference to be shared when a particular problem arises in writing. Using my story to focus instruction sets the stage for accepting constructive criticism in a workshop environment where we are working together and helping each other to become better writers. In a follow-up lesson, for example, we fine-tune our beginning sentences to make them grab readers' attention. We always make revisions to my story before inviting student volunteers to share their own stories.

I kick off our discussion with a short story of my own rotten blonde-haired older brother who once, accidentally on purpose, lodged a dart in my ankle at the neighborhood carnival. Not much prodding is needed to get students talking about the time a sibling, cousin, or friend caused an accident of some kind from stitches, bumps on heads, to—as in my brother's case—a scolding and an ice pack.

As students talk about their memorable episodes, I record the main ideas on the board. Together, we turn these ideas into titles that follow the pattern of Patricia Polacco's *Rotten Redheaded Older Brother*—with surprising results. Students are anxious to begin working on getting these stories down on paper—with a few added embellishments! Here is a sampling of our titles:

> *My Rotten Blonde-Haired Older Brother* by Mrs. L.
> *My Really, Really Rotten Little Sister with Green Eyes* by Annie
> *My Crazy Little Cousin* by Chris
> *My Really Funny Best Friend* by Sydney
> *My Not-So-Big But Bad Brother with Brown Hair Bit Me* by Jenny
> *Amanda's Punky Little Brother Paul* by Amanda

All the Places to Love
by Patricia MacLachlan

LEARNING ABOUT **Describing Places**

On the day I was born
My grandmother wrapped me in a blanket
made from the wool of her sheep.
She held me up in the open window
So that what I heard first was the wind.
What I saw first were all the places to love:
The valley,
The river falling down over rocks,
The hilltop where the blueberries grew.

— From *All the Places to Love*, page 5–6

Rich Vocabulary

tradition *n.* something that is done over and over again as part of a routine

---

Compare the poetic text and stirring illustrations of this book with the Patricia Polacco's rib-jabbing tale of sibling rivalry, *My Rotten Redheaded Older Brother.* The comparisons will create an engaging discussion. The stories have the following elements in common:

1. Each is told by a child.
2. A grandparent(s) plays a role in the day-to-day life of the main character.
3. They take place in rural settings.
4. They portray special family traditions.
5. They emit a feeling of closeness, love, and family warmth.
6. They are about fond memories.

While both of these reflective stories will inspire beginning writers to put pencils to paper, the resulting stories will have very different tones. After sharing *All the Places to Love* for read-aloud, make a list of the main characters' favorite places to love and how the text shows this. Papa, for instance, loves the fields: "'Where else is the soil so sweet?' he said."

Then ask students to make predictions about baby Sylvie, who is born on the day the story is

The Place I Love by Annie

being told. What will her favorite place be? Eli knows he will someday carry his sister on his shoulders through the fields and tell her of all the places to love: "'Where else, I WILL SAY, does an old turtle crossing the path/Make all the difference in the world?'"

With Patricia MacLachlan's words still in their minds, tell students to close their eyes and picture the place they love best. Urge them to think about what they would see, hear, smell, touch, and feel there. Pass out writing paper for students to write a reflective paragraph describing how this place can be put into words with images that show what they love best. Display students' writing on an All the Places We Love bulletin board.

....

Sophie Skates
by Rachel Isadora

LEARNING ABOUT   Writing Captions

Sophie started skating when she was three years old, on the pond behind her house. Now Sophie is eight years old. She dreams of becoming a professional ice skater, but she knows there will be many years of hard work ahead.

— From *Sophie Skates*, pages 3–4

In *Sophie Skates*, Rachel Isadora showcases a day in the life of Sophie, an eight-year-old girl working hard to reach her dream of becoming a professional skater. After skating lessons that begin at 5:00 A.M., Sophie goes to school and then returns to the rink for private lessons or attends a ballet class before going home for dinner. At this young age, she has a clearly defined goal, is motivated and disciplined to reach this goal, and is not letting the hard work intimidate her.

Share *Sophie Skates* with your second graders prior to a writers' workshop to get them thinking of a dream or a talent they would like to pursue. There is a lot of information in this story for readers to take in. Revisit the book during the work-

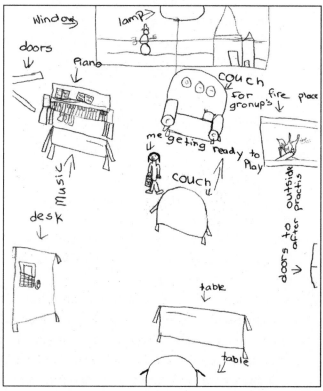

Sydney plays piano.

shop to demonstrate different methods for describing familiar experiences. In *Sophie Skates*, the illustrations include captions that add details about skating basics, moves, clothing, and more to the main text.

Have your students make an illustration that details their talents or dreams for their future. They should include captions to describe the places, events, persons, and/or objects in the picture. A few sentences of text may also be included to highlight the main idea of the illustration and supporting captions.

···

The Amazing Bone
by William Steig

 **LEARNING ABOUT** Synonyms

. . . Later [Pearl] sat on the ground in the forest between school and home, and spring was so bright and beautiful, the warm air touched her so tenderly, she could almost feel herself changing into a flower. Her light dress felt like petals.

"I love everything," she heard herself say.

"So do I," a voice answered.

Pearl straightened up and looked around. No one was there.

"Where are you?" she asked.

"Look down," came the answer. Pearl looked down.

"I'm the bone in the violets near the tree by the rock on your right."

— From *The Amazing Bone*, pages 7–8

Pearl can't wait to take her new friend home to meet her parents. Unfortunately, a sly fox, who isn't afraid of a talking bone, wants her to join him for dinner—as the main course! But luckily for Pearl, the bone used to belong to a witch from whom it learned a few magic tricks. With a "Yibbam! Yibbamsibibble! Jibrakken sibibble digray," the fox is reduced to the size of a mouse. Pearl takes her amazing bone home where her new friend is welcomed into the family.

The story of *The Amazing Bone*, like all of William Steig books, is a favorite among second graders. His animal characters get themselves into the most unusual predicaments, but somehow, amazingly, they outwit their adversaries. And, to young children's delight, they do so without any adult intervention.

The vocabulary used in Steig's books is never overused or simple; on the contrary—his word choices encourage young listeners and readers to expand their personal vocabularies of written and spoken words by his example.

Following a read-aloud of the book, share the words below to give students a taste of the unlimited choices of words available to make stories more exciting. Then have each student revisit a completed writers' workshop story, and substitute more exciting synonyms that paint pictures of what is happening in the story. Overused words like *said*, *walked*, and *looked* get a break in this activity that sharpens young writers' awareness of words.

Words That Paint Pictures in *The Amazing Bone*

William Steig could have written:	But instead, he wrote:
It was a sunny day	*It was a brilliant day*
Pearl took her time	*Pearl dawdled*
Pearl stood looking	*Pearl stood gawking*
Pearl said	*Pearl murmured*
Pearl would surprise them	*Pearl would flabbergast them*
Who should come out	*Who should rush out*
one said	*one commanded*
He looked into Pearl's purse	*He peered into Pearl's purse*
He pushed Pearl	*He shoved Pearl*
said the fox	*signed the fox*

....

When Jessie Came Across the Sea
by Amy Hest

 **LEARNING ABOUT**
Descriptive Language

When Jessie is chosen by the rabbi to make the long journey to America, she must leave her beloved grandmother behind. Jessie, brave beyond her years, saves every coin she makes sewing, and in a few years has enough money to buy her grandmother a ticket to join her in America. When Grandmother arrives in America, she discovers Jessie is now a successful seamstress who has fallen in love.

Rich Vocabulary

tattered *adj.* torn to pieces

Read aloud this touching story—and be prepared for happy tears when Jessie and her grandmother are reunited. Discuss this story of courage and hope, and explain that Amy Hest's story describes the heritage of America: Millions of children like Jessie left behind everyone and everything they knew to seek a better life in America "where the streets are paved with gold."

Following the read-aloud, feature this book in a writers' workshop lesson that explores author Amy Hest's writing style. Highlight sentences with descriptive language to demonstrate the power of adding just a few more words.

a tiny silver box

warmed thin soup

ginger-colored freckles

almond eyes

soft lace

splintered crate

tall, tall buildings that touched the sky

bright hair

soft, sweet voice

yellow chair

delicate sash

breezy day

shaky handwriting

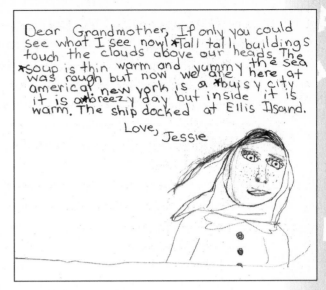

Just a few more words

Have students put themselves in Jessie's shoes as she walks onto the ship, thinks of her grandmother back in the tiny house eating thin soup alone, arrives in the crowded streets of New York, and begins a new life in a world where even the language is unfamiliar.

Encourage them to give descriptive writing a try by writing a letter to Grandmother or a journal entry detailing the feelings, sights, and experiences of Jessie's journey and arrival in America. Have students highlight sentences in which they've added just a few more words and share them during writers' workshop.

So You Want to Be President
by Judith St. George

 **Writing a Speech**

"Tall, short, fat, thin, talkative, quiet, vain, humble, lawyer, teacher, or soldier," our presidents have come in all shapes, sizes, temperaments, and skills. Just think, one of the second graders sitting in your class might grow up to be the leader of our great nation. Imagine that! Sophie aspired to be a professional skater—why shouldn't students dream of becoming president?

Share this 2001 Caldecott Medal book, and highlight the qualities your students possess that make them potential presidential material. Are they honest? Are they topnotch in the brains department? Do they have pets or pesky brothers and sisters? Are they named James, John, William, or George? If they answer yes to these and other questions posted in *So You Want to Be President*, the odds are in their favor for living in the White House someday.

> **Rich Vocabulary**
>
> **succeeded** *v.* did what you set out to do

After discussing the book, have each student write a speech announcing his or her candidacy for the presidency of the United States. This speech should convince voters of all the worthy qualities students possess that make them the best candidate to be our leader. A self-portrait should accompany the speech, which may be shared and edited and then displayed in the hallway. After students give their speeches on election day, call on them one at a time to vote by secret ballot, which will be handed out by an election official (perhaps a third grader or parent volunteer could help with this ten-minute project). Tally the votes, and announce the winner during writers' workshop. The newly elected President gets to be first in line, is never left alone, and is not required to eat broccoli (or another food) at lunch for a day.

Campaign speeches on election day

Berlioz the Bear
by Jan Brett

LEARNING ABOUT
Writing a Newspaper Article

Zum. Zum buzzz. Zum. Zum. Buzz.
Berlioz had been practicing for weeks, and now just when the orchestra was going to play in the village square for a gala ball, a strange buzz was coming from his double bass.
"Why now?" Berlioz said to himself.
— From *Berlioz the Bear*, page 3

Whatever will Berlioz do? Not only is there a strange sound coming from inside his bass, his mule has chosen this crucial time to be stubborn and refuse to pull the musicians to the ball. The pressure is on to get the mule moving. In exquisite Bavarian-style illustrations, Jan Brett includes beautifully detailed borders that tell a second story and foreshadow without words. As those in charge of the ball ready the stage for the performers and arrange food, seating, and make other preparations, Berlioz's band is joined one by one by boasting animals certain they can get the mule moving. But the rooster, cat, schnauzer, billy goat, plow horse, and ox are unsuccessful at budging the stubborn animal. Suddenly, all attention is on Berlioz's buzzing bass as a

Rich Vocabulary

disturbed *v.*
bothered

very angry bee flies out and stings the hindquarters of the mule. The little bee accomplishes what the other animals could not; Berlioz and his band of performers arrive just in time for their performance.

Share this must-have read-aloud, and then use it as a springboard for informational writing that describes the gala ball. Bring in newspaper articles for students to examine, and point out that an article should tell the following things about an event: Who, What, Where, and When. Read the following sentence, and ask students to think about what happened next:

> *The audience roared. "What an entrance!" they cried, and the orchestra, already dressed and tuned, began to play . . .*

Brainstorm a list of things that could be featured in a newspaper article about the event. Invite students to select one to write about. Have them include the sounds, sights, and smells so readers can relive the event through the words on the page. You may also wish to write a short report of Berlioz's Band Performance with students prior to independent writing time.

MORE FUN WITH THE BOOK
Let students expand their imaginations and write articles about performances by Berlioz at other places, including
- a park
- a football game
- a soccer game
- the opening of a new restaurant
- a birthday party
- a swimming pool party
- a classroom during a special event

The Wednesday Surprise
by Eve Bunting

LEARNING ABOUT   **Journaling**

I like surprises. But the one Grandma and I are planning for Dad's birthday is the best surprise of all. We work on it Wednesday nights. On Wednesdays Mom has to stay late at the office and my brother, Sam, goes to basketball practice at the Y. That's when Grandma rides the bus across town to stay with me.

— From *The Wednesday Surprise*, page 5

Rich Vocabulary

astonished *adj.*
greatly surprised

On Wednesday nights, Grandma brings a big bag of books and, when Anna and Grandma are left alone, they read for an hour, take a break for ice cream, and then read some more. When several Wednesday nights have passed, they are ready to give Dad his birthday surprise. After Dad's favorite pot roast dinner, the family gathers for gifts. Anna and Grandma save theirs for last. When Anna brings out the bag of books, Grandma reads aloud to her family for the first time. Anna, "smart as paint," has taught her grandmother how to read.

Writing a *The Wednesday Surprise* memoir

Share *The Wednesday Surprise* for a heartwarming, inspiring story with a surprise ending any day of the week. Second graders will be anxious to talk about this book and will be impressed with Anna's accomplishment. Following the read-aloud, have students write a memoir of this special day in a journal entry for Grandma or Anna. Ask pairs of students to evaluate each other's memoirs and make suggestions to the author. After the final revision, writers can add watercolor pictures to illustrate the memorable day.

Even More Must-Have Thought-Provoking Books to Spark Writing

My Ol' Man by Patricia Polacco

The Keeping Quilt by Patricia Polacco

Three Names by Patricia MacLachlan

Amazing Grace by Mary Hoffman

My Great Aunt Arizona by Gloria Houston

Bea and Mr. Jones by Amy Schwartz

Those Summers by Aliki Brandenberg

Charlie Anderson by Barbara Abercrombie

A Picnic in October by Eve Bunting

Nana Upstairs and Nana Downstairs by Tomie dePaola

Lilly at the Ballet by Rachel Isadora

Basket Moon by Mary Lyn Ray

Twilight Comes Twice by Ralph Fletcher

Chapter 4: Fairy Tale Favorites
10 Must-Have Books for
Exploring Literary Elements

Chapter Learning Goals:
* identifying main characters, settings, sequence, and problems in stories
* comparing similarities and differences in retellings of the same text
* recognizing the main ideas or themes of a story
* implementing reading skills and strategies to understand and interpret a variety of literary texts
* becoming familiar with a variety of traditional and non-traditional fairy tales

What do you get when you combine *Cinderella, Little Red Riding Hood, Princess Furball,* and *Goldilocks and the Three Bears* with *The Frog Prince Continued, The True Story of the 3 Little Pigs!,* and *Strega Nona*? A chapter of traditional and non-traditional fairy tales.

Read Jan Brett's and James Marshall's traditional and non-traditional versions of *Goldilocks and the Three Bears* for an introduction to literary elements. Chart the main characters and events of *The Three Little Pigs,* and then hand the stage over to the little "hams" in your class for a performance of this favorite tale. Challenge students to present evidence to support or disprove *The True Story of the 3 Little Pigs!*

Write a class chain-of-events story based on Steven Kellogg's *Chicken Little.* Compare the traits of the main characters in *Cinderella* and *Princess Furball* using a Venn diagram. Have students formulate a plan to outwit a wolf in *Lon Po Po,* and encourage them to identify the main theme of *The Frog Prince Continued.* Borrow Tomie dePaola's original tale of *Strega Nona* for students to retell in their own way.

Share the memorable must-have books and activities in this chapter, and your second graders will be retelling, rereading, comparing, and interpreting these once-upon-a-time tales.

---

10 Must-Have Books for Exploring Literary Elements

Goldilocks and the Three Bears retold and illustrated by Jan Brett

Goldilocks and the Three Bears retold and illustrated by James Marshall

The Three Little Pigs retold and illustrated by James Marshall

The True Story of the 3 Little Pigs! by Jon Scieszka

Chicken Little by Steven Kellogg

Cinderella retold by Barbara Karlin

Princess Furball by Charlotte Huck

Lon Po Po by Ed Young

The Frog Prince Continued by Jon Scieszka

Strega Nona by Tomie dePaola

Goldilocks and the Three Bears

retold and illustrated by Jan Brett
retold and illustrated by James Marshall

LEARNING ABOUT Story Elements

These two very different versions of the same fairy tale provoke a wonderful discussion of literary elements that will lay the groundwork and provide the vocabulary for future fairy tale book discussions. Brett's traditional and beautifully detailed once-upon-a-time tale is told with predictable "fairy tale" language; Marshall's comical, non-traditional retelling begins with the neighbors complaining that sweet little Goldilocks "isn't what she appears to be." These obviously contrasting versions allow second graders to easily compare the tales in a flowing discussion that explores different settings, main characters, themes, and events.

To prepare for this lesson, I create a Fairy Tale Characteristics chart based on the reproducible on page 74. I also make a copy of the reproducible for each student.

Then students meet me for a lesson that explores the genre of fairy tales with a traditional and non-traditional retelling by two talented and favorite authors. In the mini-lesson that follows, *Goldilocks and the Three Bears* kick offs our exploration of literary elements.

Rich Vocabulary

charming *adj.* pleasing to see

demand *v.* to order

gruff *adj.* rough or not pleasing

Mrs. L.:	Some of my all-time favorite books are retellings of favorite fairy tales.
Carrie:	Like *Hansel and Gretel*.
Hannah:	I like *Little Red Riding Hood*.
Allison:	My favorite is *Goldilocks*.
Mrs. L.:	Today we're going to take a closer look at two versions of *Goldilocks and the Three Bears* to compare how two of our favorite authors retell the same story. On this big Fairy Tale Characteristics chart, I've listed some things that make fairy tales different from other stories. Let's take a closer look at *Goldilocks and the Three Bears* by Jan Brett and *Goldilocks and the Three Bears* by James Marshall to find out what makes a fairy tale a fairy tale.
Chris:	The first column is for the title, author, and illustrator.
Mrs. L.:	Right. All stories have a title, an author, and usually, an illustrator, but fairy tales have been told so many times that the book you are reading is more than likely a retelling of the original story. On the covers of both Goldilocks books are the words *retold and illustrated by* followed by the author-illustrator's names.
Kristen:	Jan Brett and James Marshall.
Mrs. L.:	Right. Let's write the titles and authors-illustrators of the books in the first column.
Jake:	The next column is for setting.
Mrs. L:	The setting of the story is when and where it takes place. When and where does Jan Brett's version of *Goldilocks* take place?
Abby:	It happened a long time ago.
David:	In a cabin in the woods.
Mrs. L.:	How do you know this story took place long ago?
Sydney:	Nobody dresses that way anymore.
Matthew:	Bears don't wear clothes at all. I think that's the way they dress in another country. But it still looks more like a long time ago.
Mrs. L.:	Let's write "long ago in a cabin in the woods" under setting. What about the setting for James Marshall's *Goldilocks and the Three Bears*? I'll skim through the pages and show you. Look at this page where Goldilocks is lying in the biggest bear's bed.
Carrie:	I have bunny slippers just like the ones beside the bed so it has to be happening today.
Luke:	And there's a light on the night stand. There's electricity!
Kristen:	It's definitely more today than the other Goldilocks.
Annie:	The place is still a cabin in the woods—or a house.
Mrs. L.:	A "charming" house I remember reading. Let's write "today in a charming house in the woods." What's the next column?
Jenny:	Once upon a time . . . That's how all fairy tales start.
Mrs. L.:	Here's Jan Brett's beginning: "Once upon a time there were three bears who lived together in a house of their own in a wood."
Jenny:	We should write "yes" for Jan Brett's *Goldilocks* since it starts out with "once upon a time."

Mrs. L.:	Good thinking. Now let's try out James Marshall's beginning: "Once there was a little girl called Goldilocks. 'What a sweet child,' said someone new in town. 'That's what you think,' said a neighbor."
Jesse:	That would be a no.
Jenny:	That means not all fairy tales start out this way. And they don't all end with "happily every after."
Mrs. L.:	Right. Which Goldilocks do you think will end "happily ever after?"
Matthew:	Jan Brett's.
Mrs. L.:	Let's check. "And what happened to Goldilocks afterwards, no one can tell. But the three bears never saw anything more of her."
Michael:	It's not "happily ever after."
Mrs. L.:	Not exactly.
Allison:	But since the bears never saw her again, you can guess they were happy.
Kristen:	It doesn't have to say "happily ever after." Look at the picture. You can see they're happy. They're giving each other a big hugs—that sure is happy!
Mrs. L.:	Good thinking. Maybe Jan Brett wanted you to see for yourself that they will live "happily ever after" from the picture. Let's check out James Marshall's ending.
David:	It definitely won't say "happily ever after."
Mrs. L.:	Let's read it: "'Who was that little girl?' asked Baby Bear. 'I have no idea,' said Mama Bear. 'But I hope we never see her again.' And they never did.'"
Jan:	No "happily ever after" in this one, either.
Mrs. L.:	We'll write "no" for both in this column. The beginnings and endings also help us answer the next part of our chart, which is traditional or non-traditional. The word we use to describe the tales like Jan Brett's Goldilocks is *traditional*. Traditional fairy tales take place long ago, begin "once upon a time," and usually end "happily ever after." James Marshall's retellings are non-traditional. He retells the story and gives it a present-day twist.
Chris:	Should we write these words down?
Mrs. L.:	Yes. Jan Brett's retelling is . . .
Class:	Traditional.
Mrs. L.:	And James Marshall's retelling is . . .
Class:	Not traditional.
Mrs. L.:	Right, or non-traditional. Now we need to talk about the characters in fairy tales.
George:	The three bears are the good characters.
Carrie:	Goldilocks is the bad one.
Allison:	She's not bad, she's curious.
Mrs. L.:	I agree. How about if we write "Goldilocks" under bad character but then we'll write "curious" in parentheses?
David:	Well, it was bad for her to go into a stranger's house.
Michael:	I don't think she'll do that again. She learned a lesson at the end of the story.
Mrs. L.:	Another name for the lesson of the story is the moral of the story. Fairy tales often have morals. Morals help teach you proper ways to behave. Let's write "Goldilocks" and "three bears" under bad and good characters. Then write

Teaching With Favorite Read-Alouds in Second Grade

"don't go into strangers' houses" under moral of the story, at the end of our chart. Are there any other main characters in these two versions of *Goldilocks*? Look at the pictures while I skim through them.

Timothy: There aren't any in Jan Brett's book.

Dean: There are some neighbors and Goldilock's mother.

Mrs. L.: Are these main characters?

Class: No.

Jenny: Just extras.

Mrs. L.: Then let's write "none" under Other Fairy Tale Characters. Some fairy tales have a fairy godmother or a dragon in them. Others have kings and queens and princes and princesses. Magic is another characteristic of lots of fairy tales.

Timothy: The bears could talk—is this magic?

Mrs. L.: No, but this certainly is a special quality of the story. Many stories have animals that can talk to make the story more exciting.

Jan: Like in *Sylvester and the Magic Pebble*.

Annie: And *Jack and the Beanstalk* has magic beans.

Mrs. L.: Good remembering! Is there any magic in *Goldilocks and the Three Bears*?

Class: No.

Sydney: But there is three of something. That's the next column on the chart.

Mrs. L.: Right. Let's write "bears" under Threes. There are more threes in this story, too . . .

Luke: Three chairs.

Maggie: Three bowls of porridge.

Jesse: Beds.

Mrs. L.: Let's add "bears, chairs, bowls, and beds" under threes. Can you think of any other fairy tale that has a three in the title?

George: *The Three Little Pigs*.

Dean: *The Three Wishes*. There are three musicians in that one, too.

Mrs. L.: Wow! You certainly know your fairy tales. Let's read over our completed fairy tale characteristic chart.

Fairy Tale Characteristics Chart

Title, Author, Illustrator	Setting: Time & Place	Once upon a time . . .	Traditional or Non-traditional	"Good" Characters	"Bad" Characters	Other Characters	Magic used	Threes	...happily ever after	Moral of the story
Goldilocks and the Three Bears by Jan Brett	long ago in a cabin in the woods	yes	traditional	three bears	Goldilocks (curious)	none	no	bears chairs bowls beds	no	don't go into strangers' houses
Goldilocks and the Three Bears by James Marshall	today in a charming house in the woods	no	non-traditional	three bears	Goldilocks (curious)	none	no	bears chairs bowls beds	no	don't go into strangers' house

Each time you share a new fairy tale, add its characteristics to your chart. Soon it will be filled with the results of your literary discussions as the children grow more familiar with fairy tales and authors' styles.

More Goldilocks Read-Aloud Fun

Dusty Locks and the Three Bears by Susan Lowell

Somebody and the Three Blairs by Marilyn Tolhurst

More Must-Have Books for Exploring Literary Elements

....

The Three Little Pigs
retold and illustrated by James Marshall

LEARNING ABOUT **Characters And Events**

The cover of Marshall's book depicts the three little pigs taking a bow after their performance of this tale. Give the little "hams" in your class a stage on which to perform using Marshall's version as a guide and a few simple props.

Begin with a director's meeting where the class charts the main characters and events in the story. The beginning of our charted version looks something like this non-traditional retelling of this tale.

The three little pigs leave home.
The first little pig builds a house of straw.
The big bad wolf blows down the little pig's house and gobbles him up.

The second little pig builds a house of sticks.
The big bad wolf blows down the little pig's house and gobbles him up.

The third little pig builds a house of bricks.
The big bad wolf tries to blow down the little pig's house but can't . . .

Next divide the class into three production groups to create backdrops depicting the setting of the little pig's houses. For instance, the "stick house group" could glue small twigs to its home; the "straw house group" could attach plastic drinking straws or pieces of hay to its home; and the "brick house group" could outline bricks on pieces of sandpaper and then paint them red.

Provide time for each group to practice retelling and acting out their part of the story. Encourage them to write a script to help them learn their parts. Hold a dress rehearsal for a kindergarten audience before an opening night (or afternoon) performance for parents.

Rich Vocabulary

muttered *v.* talked in a way that is hard to understand

The True Story of the 3 Little Pigs!
by Jon Scieszka

LEARNING ABOUT   Making Inferences

Give your students a lesson in hearing both sides of the story after sharing this book. Cast one student as the wolf, and another as the surviving pig. Let the rest of the students act as the jury and listen to Alexander's version of what happened that fateful day when he allegedly went to borrow a cup of sugar from his neighbors, the three little pigs.

Be sure to have Alexander and the third little pig sworn in before testifying; the students playing these parts can lay their hands on a book of fairy tales and promise to "tell the whole truth and nothing but the truth so help us all in once-upon-a-time land."

Prior to the trial, peruse the illustrations with students so they can build their case for or against the wolf. My class inferred the following pieces of evidence:

1. A.T. Wolf likes to eat cute fuzzy animals. There are mouse parts and bunny ears in his cheeseburger; there are bunny ears in his granny's birthday cake.
2. The picture of his granny hanging on the wall looks like she's the wolf posing as Little Red Riding Hood's Granny and we know how "sweet" she was!
3. The broken house of sticks formed a spoon, knife, and fork beside the second little pig.
4. How trustworthy is "wolf's honor," anyway?
5. The third little pig had every right to say, "Get out of here, Wolf. Don't bother me again." The wolf had just eaten his brothers.
6. Alexander admitted he went a little crazy and made a real scene when the third pig said his old granny could sit on a pin.
7. Alexander admits that he ate the first two little pigs but claims they were already "dead as doornails."

Although the evidence is compelling against the wolf, ask students to examine it in a way that is more favorable to him. Was there a bout of "swine fever" or a tornado in the area? Were substandard building techniques utilized in the construction of the first two pigs' homes? Can mother wolf or mother pig be called to testify?

After students practice their parts, invite the principal in to give a brief lecture on telling the truth and being a responsible jury member. Acting as the judge, he or she should ask the jury to vote. The principal will also have the honor of reading aloud the verdict.

Rich Vocabulary

scene *n.* when someone causes a fuss or draws attention to a certain event

---

MORE FUN WITH THE BOOK

After sharing other versions of *The Three Little Pigs* for read-aloud, I display the books in a line and ask students to choose their favorite by stacking a Unifix cube below their choice. Following our discussion of this graph, I invite students to bring in their own versions of *The Three Little Pigs* from home. During sharing time, we sort the books by criteria such as whether or not the wolf met his demise at the end and whether the story is traditional or non-traditional. Then we set up a reading corner featuring these books.

Our Favorite Three Little Pigs

···

Chicken Little
by Steven Kellogg

LEARNING ABOUT   ## Cause and Effect

Disguising his poultry truck as a "poulice" van, Foxy Loxy ventures out to assist a gang of hysterical birds. An acorn has landed on Chicken Little's head, causing her to think the sky is falling. Foxy Loxy, in his haste to use the "foolish fowl" in his favorite poultry recipes, makes the tragic error of hurling the acorn into sky. The acorn becomes lodged in the propeller of a sky patrol helicopter being flown by Sergeant Hippo Hefty of the "hippolice." As the helicopter comes careening into the poultry truck, Foxy Loxy screams, "THE SKY IS FALLING!" And in fact, this time it was. The word *sky* painted on the side of the helicopter is heading straight for Foxy Loxy. Sergeant Hefty tumbles from the sky, lands flat on top of Foxy Loxy, and shouts, "You're under arrest." "You mean I'm under a fat hippo," snaps Foxy Loxy.

Second graders love these word plays, and giggles abound when Steven Kellogg's hilarious retelling of Chicken Little's near mishap with friends Turkey Lurkey, Ducky Lucky, Gosling Gilbert, Goosey Loosey, and even Henny Penny is shared.

After reading this story, take a closer look at the clever details in the illustrations. Turkey Lurkey's muscle shirt with the words *Big Bozo's Barnyard Gym* on it and Goosey Loosey's karate suit prove that they're "tough birds." And when Foxy Loxy can't resist sharing the recipes he's "selected for each of his captives," the illustration shows the cookbook

Rich Vocabulary
horrified *adj.* terrified, scared

open to a table of contents that includes recipes for chicken salad, southern fried chicken, broiled duck in spicy sauce, toasted gosling, poached goose, and roast turkey.

Following the read-aloud and discussion, use the chain reaction of main events beginning with the acorn hitting Chicken Little on the head and ending with her telling her grandchildren about that day when the sky fell. Use the cause-and-effect pattern from the familiar *If You Give a Mouse a Cookie* by Laura Numeroff to retell the story of Chicken Little.

If an acorn falls on Chicken Little's head, she might think the sky is falling.
If she thinks the sky is falling, she'll probably run and tell her friends.
When she's talking to her friends, a fox might overhear.
When the fox sees Chicken Little telling the story to her feathered friends, he'll remember his
    favorite poultry recipes.
Thinking about poultry will make him think of "poulice."
Thinking of police will give him the idea to disguise himself like a policeman and try to trick
    Chicken Little into taking a ride in his "poulice" truck.
When Chicken Little and her friends are piling into the truck, he'll laugh and show them the acorn
    that hit her on the head.
He'll throw the acorn into the air.
Throwing the acorn into the air just might cause it to lodge into the propeller of a sky patrol helicopter.
When the acorn lodges in the propeller, the helicopter will come crashing to the ground.
When the sky patrol is crashing to the ground, the hippoliceman will fall with it.
When the hippoliceman falls to the ground, he just might land on Foxy Loxy and arrest him.
After he's arrested, he'll have a trial to see if he's guilty or innocent.
Chicken Little and her friends will testify at the trial.
On her way home from trial, Chicken Little might recover the acorn that first hit her on the head.
If she plants the acorn next to her coop, she'll someday have an oak tree.
And chances are, years later, she'll snuggle under the tree with her grandchildren and tell them about
    the day the sky was falling.

Record students' ideas on sentence strips, and then ask them to illustrate each line with a simple picture and an arrow linking one event in the story to the next.

MORE FUN WITH THE BOOK

- Make posters of Chicken Little's lessons, such as "Never trust a fox dressed like a policeman—ask for identification" or "Don't get hysterical in an emergency—remain calm!"
- Create wanted posters for Foxy Loxy using the title page of Kellogg's book as an example.
- Write newspaper articles or special TV and radio reports highlighting Foxy Loxy's apprehension by Sergeant Hippo.
- Give students extra writing practice by putting together a book entitled *Favorite Chicken Little Recipes*. Students write about how they think their favorite chicken recipe is prepared. Send finished recipe cards home for adults to "try" or at least have a laugh! The recipe to the right is a sample from my class.

> **Maggies Chikin Wings**
> By a pac of chikin wings.
> Poor sum hot pepprs and a jar of sos (like spugety) over the chikin.
> Poor in a pan.
> Put in a HOT ovin and bak for 3 ourrs I thik.
> Hav a glas of woter wn you eat—your moth may catch on fir!

Cinderella

retold by Barbara Karlin

Describing Characters

This non-traditional version of *Cinderella* retold by Barbara Karlin and illustrated with true James Marshall-esque humor adds two lizards and a rat to the royal court, as well as a plump little woman as the fairy godmother. Following her wedding to the prince, this generous and forgiving Cinderella moves her whole family—and the fairy godmother—into the palace and finds a lord of the court for each of her stepsisters to marry.

Share this version for read-aloud, and then bring the book back to a lesson on using words to describe characters. Make a copy of the Venn diagram on

Rich Vocabulary

ridiculous *adj.* such a different idea that it's not even possible

page 75 for each student. As you reread the book, ask students to record words that describe her character in the circle labeled *Cinderella*. *Hardworking, nice, miserable, brave, generous*, and *forgiving* are all words used in the story to describe this Cinderella. Complete the Venn diagram after a read-aloud and discussion of *Princess Furball* (see below).

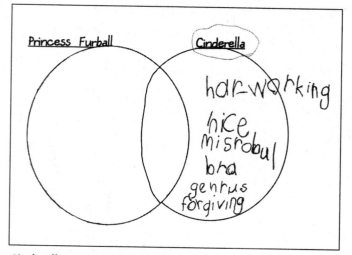

Cinderella section of Venn diagram

Princess Furball

by Charlotte Huck

Making Comparisons

Princess Furball, with its thousand-furs motif, is a variant of the French *Cinderella* tale and its glass slipper ending. When her father promises her hand in marriage in exchange for 50 wagons full of silver, the princess demands three beautiful dresses as wedding gifts first—and a coat made of a thousand different kinds of fur. When the gifts are amazingly produced, Princess Furball's plan to prevent the wedding falls apart and she is forced to run away.

Share this story for read-aloud, and then compare it to the non-traditional retelling of *Cinderella* by Barbara Karlin. Discuss the following information about Princess Furball and Cinderella:

- *They worked very hard as servants.*
- *They appeared at balls as beautiful, unknown princesses.*
- *They danced with princes or kings and then mysteriously disappeared from sight.*
- *They left objects behind that fit them (a glass slipper, a golden ring).*
- *They married their princes or kings and lived happily ever after.*

Have students use the Venn diagram from the previous activity to record words describing Princess Furball such as *clever, lovely, brave,* and *charming*. Show students how to draw lines to the center of the Venn diagram to show the characteristics that describe both Cinderella and Princess Furball.

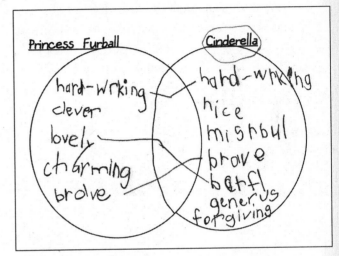

Completed Venn diagram

Lon Po Po
by Ed Young

LEARNING ABOUT Making Predictions

In this beautifully illustrated Red Riding Hood tale from China, three sisters, Shang, Tao and Paotze, learn the importance of obeying their mother. When Mother leaves to visit Grandmother—their Po Po—her final words are a reminder to "close the door tight at sunset and latch it well."

When an old wolf posing as their Po Po knocks on the door, it takes a cunning plan to outwit him. Shang, the sharpest and eldest of the three sisters, becomes suspicious of Po Po's identity when she catches a glimpse of the wolf's hairy face before a candle is blown out. She quickly formulates a plan to save her sisters and herself.

Read aloud *Lon Po Po*, but close the book after reading page 15. Ask students to predict what they think will happen next. Then have them work in teams to formulate plans to save the sisters from the wolf. Meet as a full group to share plans for outfoxing the wolf before revealing Ed Young's ending. Here are some of my students' suggestions.

How to Outwit the Wolf

- Paint spots on yourself with a marker and claim to have a contagious disease that is fatal. The first symptom is being very hungry.
- Lock the wolf into a closet or another room—tell him there's a birthday present for Po Po that he must find. Then push a heavy piece of furniture against the door. Quickly call 911 or run to a neighbor's house for help.
- Tell the wolf you want to surprise him with a special dinner. Put a blindfold on him and then rush to a neighbor's house for help.
- Send one sister out the window to pretend to be the real Po Po. She knocks on the door to scare the wolf away. If that doesn't work, have her run for help.

· ·

The Frog Prince Continued
by Jon Scieszka

 **LEARNING ABOUT** Theme

The Princess kissed the frog,
He turned into a Prince.
And they lived happily ever after . . .
— From *The Frog Prince Continued*, page 5

The prince can't understand why he and his princess aren't living happily ever after. Then one day in a fit of rage, the princess wonders aloud, "Sometimes I think we would both be better off if you were still a frog." So, the prince runs off to find a witch to turn him back into a frog. Although the Frog Prince meets the witches from *Sleeping Beauty*, *Snow White*, and *Hansel and Gretel*, the fairy godmother from *Cinderella* turns him into . . . a beautiful carriage. Just as the prince fears he will certainly live unhappily ever after, a clock strikes midnight, and he turns back into his princely self. He rushes back to the castle and discovers the princess has been worried sick about him. On the last page, it is clear the prince and princess have again found true love.

> **Rich Vocabulary**
>
> **nagged** *v.* repeated the same thing in an annoying way

The Prince kissed the Princess.
They both turned into frogs.
And they hopped off happily ever after.
The End.

After reading and discussing *The Frog Prince Continued*, display the coat of arms from the title page. Discuss how the main theme of the story is depicted in the picture of the two frogs holding hands, lips pursed in a kiss, a royal checkerboard pattern, and one blank space. Challenge students to think of the Frog Prince's tale and fill in the blank space on the coat of arms.

Have them draw the coat of arms on construction paper and add their own drawings or use pictures cut from magazines to complete the design. Perhaps a heart might be added, the pond where they enjoy each others' company, or a book based on their story.

ON ANOTHER DAY

Set up a center where students can create coats of arms to represent the main themes in other fairy tales. Cinderella, for example, might have a glass slipper, a broom, and animals that turned into her helpers at the ball; Snow White's coat of arms would probably include an apple, and the number seven for the dwarfs. Provide a pattern and paper for tracing a coat of arms shield, scrap paper, glue, magazines, crayons, and pencils. Hang completed shields on the windows of the classroom as shown in the illustration of the Frog Prince rereading his original story (page 9).

Fairy tale coat of arms

·······························

Strega Nona
by Tomie dePaola

LEARNING ABOUT

Story Elements

Bubble, bubble, pasta pot,
Boil me some pasta, nice and hot,
I'm hungry and it's time to sup,
Boil enough pasta to fill me up.
And the pasta pot bubbled and boiled and was
suddenly filled with steaming hot pasta.
— From *Strega Nona*, page 8

Unfortunately for Big Anthony, he doesn't see Strega Nona blow three kisses to the magic pasta pot to make it stop. So when he makes pasta for the whole village—despite Strega Nona's warning, the results are nearly catastrophic. Tomie dePaola's Caldecott Honor Book, *Strega Nona* has the makings of a classic fairy tale—magic, a lesson to be learned, and a once-upon-a-time setting. The 25th anniversary edition is proof that this original tale is probably being shared by a new generation of children who will in turn share it with their children, and so on, and so on.

Let your students borrow *Strega Nona* to practice retelling an original tale in a new way. Pass out paper for writers to take notes to help them organize thoughts about sequencing, main events, main characters, and setting for an accurate retelling. Reread *Strega Nona* as students listen with a writer's perspective, taking notes of things they want to remember to craft a plan for writing. After taking notes, they may copy the following title onto story writing paper and begin their retelling.

Strega Nona
an original tale by Tomie dePaola
retold by _____

Read completed stories in sharing groups to help writers assess their retellings.

Sharing *Strega Nona* retellings

More Must-Do Fairy Tale Activities

Happily Ever After Day: End your fairy tale unit with a Happily Ever After Day. Send a note home requesting that students come to school dressed as their favorite fairy tale character on a given date.

Favorite Fairy Tale Graphs: Use Happily Ever After Day to try out some graphing. Chart the following statement: My favorite fairy tale book is _____. Display the ten books featured in this chapter. Provide learning links or Unifix cubes for students to record their votes for their favorite tale. Discuss the results of the graph and pose a few more graphing questions.

Voting for a favorite fairy tale

More Fairy Tale Graph Questions: Extend your graphing lesson with the following questions:
- Which is your favorite version of *Goldilocks and the Three Bears*?
- Which is your favorite version of *The Three Little Pigs*?
- Which is your favorite version of *Little Red Riding Hood*?
- Which is your favorite version of *Cinderella*?
- Which fairy tale should I read today?
- Who is your favorite fairy tale author?
- Do you like traditional or non-traditional stories best?
- Which is your favorite retelling of a fairy tale?

Writing Fairy Tale What-Ifs: Have students write stories using what-if ideas.
What if . . .
- Goldilocks lived in outer space?
- Little Red Riding Hood's grandmother lived in the city? (She takes a cab to her house, and the Wolf is the driver . . .)
- the Three Bears confronted Goldilocks, or called her mother—or the police!
- the Three Little Pigs built their houses out of Jell-O, sand, and Legos?
- the sky really was falling on Chicken Little? (Hail!)
- Rapunzel had *just* had a haircut?
- the Frog Prince had been a toad or a chipmunk or a bear?
- the Little Red Hen's friends helped her make bread?
- the Ugly Duckling had been hatched by an ostrich?
- Hansel and Gretel took a different path and never found the candy house?

Keep Reading Happily Ever After: Just because your study of fairy tales is over doesn't mean you have to put away these books. Designate a shelf or box in your silent reading library for these newfound favorites. Keep adding to the collection as the year progresses.

Even More Must-Have Books for Exploring Literary Elements

Old Mother Hubbard and Her Wonderful Dog by James Marshall

Hansel and Gretel by James Marshall

The Three Little Wolves and the Big Bad Pig by Eugene Trivzas

The Three Sillies by Steven Kellogg

Strega Nona: Her Story by Tomie dePaola

Teaching With Favorite Read-Alouds in Second Grade

Fairy Tale Characteristics Chart

Title Author Illustrator	Setting (Time and Place)	Once upon a time…	Traditional or Non-traditional	"Good" Characters	"Bad" Characters	Other Fairy Tale Characters	Magic Used?	Threes	Happily ever after	Moral of the Story

Use with *Goldilocks and the Three Bears* retold and illustrated by Jan Brett and *Goldilocks and the Three Bears* retold and illustrated by James Marshall.

Teaching With Favorite Read-Alouds in Second Grade

Cinderella Is So . . .

Directions:

1. Listen to the story of <u>Cinderella</u> by Barbara Karlin. In the Venn diagram, write words that describe this character. Use the circle that is labeled with her name.

2. Listen to the story of <u>Princess Furball</u> by Charlotte Huck. In the Venn diagram, write words that describe this character. Use the circle that is labeled with her name.

3. Draw arrows or recopy words that describe both characters in the overlapping part of the circles.

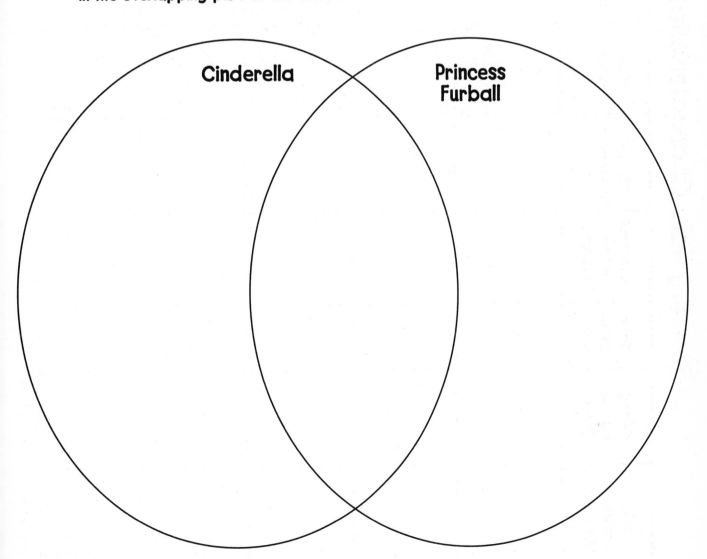

Cinderella   Princess Furball

Use with *Cinderella* by Barbara Karlin and *Princess Furball* by Charlotte Huck.

Chapter 5: Everyday Learning, Computing, Discovering
10 Must-Have Books as Springboards to Math and Science

Chapter Learning Goals:

* using problem-solving strategies to explore and solve problems
* demonstrating an understanding of number relationships given numbers to 500
* recognizing and creating patterns (2s, 5s, 10s through 500)
* recognizing and creating 5-step patterns using manipulatives
* exploring estimation skills to aid in computation
* understanding and using place value to develop number sense
* solving 2-digit addition and subtraction problems with and without regrouping
* recording and interpreting information comparing 5 or more groups on a bar graph
* identifying and combining coins to 99 cents
* telling time in 15-minute intervals
* exploring animal and fish habitats
* exploring natural resources and conservation

It's often hard for young children to understand how problem solving, computing, and scientific concepts relate to the world outside the classroom. The characters, problems, and themes of these books can motivate and show how this learning relates to children's everyday experiences.

Review the numbers to 200 with *Jumanji*. Make bar graphs to organize information based on *A Rose for Pinkerton* and *Ira Sleeps Over*. Explore patterns with *Crickwing*. Solve word problems after reading *Cloudy with a Chance of Meatballs*. Help *Alexander, Who Used to Be Rich Last Sunday* keep track of coins that add up to a dollar. Engage students in telling time in 15-minute intervals with *Harry the Dirty Dog*.

Create murals about protecting the water habitats depicted in *My Visit to the Aquarium*. Learn how to make a difference in the world based on what happens in *The Wump World*. See how an egg becomes a butterfly as pages turn in *Waiting for Wings*.

---

10 Must-Have Books as Springboards to Math and Science

Jumanji by Chris Van Allsburg

A Rose for Pinkerton by Steven Kellogg

Crickwing by Janell Cannon

Cloudy with a Chance of Meatballs by Judi Barrett

Alexander, Who Used to Be Rich Last Sunday by Judith Viorst

Ira Sleeps Over by Bernard Waber

Harry the Dirty Dog by Gene Zion

My Visit to the Aquarium by Aliki

The Wump World by Bill Peet

Waiting for Wings by Lois Ehlert

Jumanji
by Chris Van Allsburg

 **LEARNING ABOUT** Number Relationships

It was cold for November. The children could see their breath like steam. They rolled in the leaves and when Judy tried to stuff some leaves down Peter's sweater he jumped up and ran behind a tree. When his sister caught up with him, he was kneeling at the foot of the tree, looking at a long thin box. "What's that?" Judy asked. "It's a game," said Peter, handing her the box. "JUMANJI," Judy read from the box, "A JUNGLE ADVENTURE GAME."

— From *Jumanji*, page 6

It's no surprise that Chris Van Allsburg was awarded the 1982 Caldecott Medal for this book. His marvelous pictures bring to life the story of what happened the day Peter and Judy find a game in the park. Even though it looks like every other game they own, Jumanji claims to be "especially designed for the bored and restless." Peter and Judy take the game home and begin to play after reading one final warning in capital letters.

Rich Vocabulary

restless *adj.* unable to rest, "antsy"

VERY IMPORTANT: ONCE A GAME OF JUMANJI
IS STARTED IT WILL NOT BE OVER UNTIL ONE
PLAYER REACHES THE GOLDEN CITY.

What happens next proves that these two were better off being bored. As a lion, two monkeys, an eight-foot snake, and stampeding rhinos wreak havoc on the house, the children frantically play until Judy reaches the Golden City and yells, "Jumanji." They have just enough time to return the game to the park and collapse with exhaustion on the sofa before their parents come home.

Children will hang on to every word of *Jumanji*. The length of time it takes to read the text on each page provides them with time to take in the realistic illustrations. On the day after sharing *Jumanji* during read-aloud, motivate your students with the following book-based math review of numbers.

Make a transparency of the game board on page 93. Fill in the blank spaces on the gameboard with more *Jumanji* related events. Place it in a long flat box with a lid. Add a die, game pieces (we use different plastic animals), and level-appropriate math questions copied onto index cards (our review questions appear in the mini-lesson modeled below). Tape a note to the lid that reads: "Free game, guaranteed fun for all, not just some. P.S. Read instructions carefully." Print the name of the game and simple directions on the lid as follows:

JUMANJI MATH GAME
A jungle adventure game for second graders who want to improve their number skills. It's specially designed for those who like a challenge.

DIRECTIONS:
A. Group leaders place a game piece on the path in the deepest jungle.
B. A group member rolls the die and moves the game piece that number of spaces.
C. Group members work together to answer a math question in order to keep moving along the path to the city of Jumanji. If you miss a question, your group loses a turn.
D. The first group to reach Jumanji and yell the city's name aloud is the winner.
E. VERY IMPORTANT: ONCE A GAME IS STARTED IT WILL NOT BE OVER UNTIL ONE PLAYER REACHES JUMANJI, THE GOLDEN CITY.

Prior to math time, place the box in a conspicuous place where students are sure to find it. My classroom lesson began when Matthew found the game box in the silent reading corner after lunch.

Matthew: Hey! Look at the box I just found. It says, "Jumanji Math Game."
Sydney: What's the note say?
Mrs. L.:   Let's take a look. It says, "Free game, guaranteed fun for all, not just some. P.S. Read instructions carefully."
Matthew: Can we play it now?

Maggie:	We'd better not. Lions and rhinos might charge into the school.
Abby:	No, this is a math game. It's not the same Jumanji game.
Chris:	Well, we did just read *Jumanji* for read-aloud yesterday. Maybe those kids who had the game at the end of the book dropped it off while we were at lunch.
Maggie:	No, they were eaten by the lion. Their mother said they never finish games once they start them.
Jake:	And they never read instructions, either. So the lion wouldn't have gone away, and he would be hungry by now.
Mrs. L.:	What amazing imaginations you have! Come to the gathering space for math time. I'll open the box and see what's inside. Look, it's a game board trans- parency for the overhead projector. I'll set it up, and we can read the direc- tions together. *(I turn on the overhead projector, and we read the directions at the top of the page. I quickly divide students into four math groups that I've organized prior to this lesson. I also distribute scrap paper, pencils, and lapboards for computation.)*
Mrs. L.:	Sydney, Jake, Annie, and Michael are our Jumanji leaders today. Please choose a game piece for your group. We'll go in *A-B-C* order using the leaders' first names: Annie, since your name starts with *A*, your group goes first.
Annie:	I rolled a two.
Mrs. L.:	Please come up and move your game piece two spaces. What space did you land on?
Annie:	Move ahead five spaces to catch up with Guide.
Timothy:	Oh, boy! Can we move up five spaces?
Mrs. L.:	If you answer the math question correctly. Tell me which number is greater. *(I write 420 and 402 on the board.)* Talk among yourselves.
Timothy:	Four hundred twenty.
Mrs. L.:	You're right. Tell me about how you decided.
Joel:	There's a two in the tens place in four hundred twenty and a zero in the tens place in four hundred two, so four hundred twenty must be greater.
Mrs. L.:	Excellent math thinking, group. Now it's your group's turn, Jake.
Jake:	I rolled a five. It says, "Move ahead three spaces to avoid being bitten by a tsetse fly."
Mrs. L.:	I'll write a set of numbers on the board. Place them in increasing order. You can use scrap paper. *(I write 212, 220, and 122 on the board.)*
Hannah:	We're ready.
Mrs. L.:	Please write them on the board so the rest of the class can check your answer. *(Luke writes 122, 212, 220.)*
Mrs. L.:	Read the numbers for me please.
Luke:	One hundred and twenty-two, two hundred twelve, and two hundred twenty.
Mrs. L.:	Excellent! You may move ahead three spaces. Michael, go ahead and roll.
Michael:	Six. Monsoon season hits. Go back for umbrellas.
Jenny:	Looks like you'll need to answer your question or a monsoon will hit. I think you'll still have to go back for umbrellas, though.

Mrs. L.:	I think so, too. Here's your question—better put on your math thinking caps, groups: Continue the pattern. I'll write the pattern one on the board. *(I write 121, ____, 125, ____, 129, ____.)*
Allison:	We've got it. I'll write the completed pattern on the board. *(She writes the following numbers: 121, 123, 125, 127, 129, 131.)*
Mrs. L.:	What do you think, groups? Smile if you agree. Tell me about this pattern.
Jesse:	It's counting by twos so you skip the number in between each number.
Mrs. L.:	Good thinking by Michael's group. You can go back and get your umbrellas now. Sydney, it's your group's turn.
Sydney:	I rolled a two. "Move ahead five spaces to catch up with guide." We'll be tied with Annie's group!
Mrs. L.:	Here's your question: Which number is in the hundreds place? The ones place? The tens place? *(I write 153 on the board.)*
Carrie:	The one is in the hundreds place; the three is in the tens place; and the five is in the ones place.
Maggie:	No!
Mrs. L.:	Try again. You were right when you said the one is in the hundreds place.
Carrie:	The five is in the tens place, and the three is in the ones place.
Kristen:	That has to be right now.
Mrs. L.:	What do you think, class?
Class:	Yes!
Mrs. L.:	I'll get the next question ready. It's a less-than question, Annie.

(Teams continue answering questions and moving around the game board toward Jumanji, the Golden City. Our mini-lesson continues below just as Michael's team gets its third question.)

Dean:	If we get this one right we get to yell, "Jumanji."
Mrs. L.:	Think carefully. Continue this pattern. I'll write it on the board. *(I write the following numbers: 24, 28, ___, 36, ___, 44, 48.)*
George:	That's a tricky one.
Mrs. L.:	Use your scrap paper, and talk it over with your group.
Allison:	I think we have it.
Mrs. L.:	Tell me about this pattern.
Allison:	We think the pattern skips three numbers in between.
Jenny:	The first missing number is thirty-two.
Mrs. L.:	Show me how you figured this out.
Michael:	I can show you with my fingers. Say twenty-eight out loud and then put up a finger for the numbers until you get to thirty-two: twenty-nine, thirty, thirty-one. Three numbers were skipped.
Mrs. L.:	Excellent! And the fourth number, thirty-two, is the missing number. Let's keep going.
Class:	Thirty-three, thirty-four, thirty-five, thirty-six.
Mrs. L.:	Great! Keep going. *(I record the numbers on the board. To further illustrate the pattern I write the numbers so that the ones place in each column is the same.)*

Class:	Thirty-seven, thirty-eight, thirty-nine, forty. *(Michael's group shouts JUMANJI!)*
Mrs. L.:	Congratulations!
Chris:	Can we keep playing?
Mrs. L.:	I just happen to have copies of the Jumanji game board for you to play with partners. Count by fours to move through the jungle. See if you notice a new pattern as you continue to skip three numbers and write down the fourth number. Use your scrap paper for recording the pattern.

ON ANOTHER DAY

We kick off our next day's math lesson by discussing the patterns that evolved. Students identify the pattern of 4, 8, 2, 6, 0 (e.g., 24, 28, 32, 36, 40) in the ones place. Then I pass out a number grid from 100 to 200 to each student. Everyone colors in the fourth number with surprising results. One astute student noticed that the numbers changed as they went from the top to the bottom of the grid.

100	104	108	112	116	120	124	128	132	136
140	144	148	152	156	160	164	168	172	176
180	184	188	192	196	200	204	208	212	216

Counting by 4s from 100 to 200

More Must-Have Books as Springboards to Math and Science

....

A Rose for Pinkerton
by Steven Kellogg

LEARNING ABOUT Graphs

Pinkerton, are you lonely?
Do you miss curling up with your brothers and sisters?
We should get some other Great Dane puppies to play with Pinkerton …
— From *A Rose for Pinkerton*, page 4

Rich Vocabulary

intrude *v.* to get in the middle of

berserk *adj.* wild

Although Mother says one Great Dane is enough (she would prefer a small and quiet pet like a goldfish), a kitten named Rose is what the family gets. Sarah Chattercat's book says that Great Dane puppies and kittens can become good friends, but when Rose takes Pinkerton's sun spot, dog bowl, and decides she wants to be a Great Dane, Pinkerton tries to be a kitten.

Dog and cat lovers will love the story of Pinkerton and Rose. Share this story for read-aloud, allowing lots of time for children to take in Steven Kellogg's detailed illustrations. It's no surprise that Kellogg is a Great Dane owner; his portrayal of Pinkerton's expressions and feelings proves he has first-hand knowledge of canine antics. Then use the story of *A Rose for Pinkerton* as a springboard to a graphing activity.

Following the read-aloud, have children help create a graph that will organize information about their pets. We begin by brainstorming the types of pets they have and then make a bar graph to compare five groups of pet owners: dogs, cats, dogs and cats, small and quiet pets, and those without pets. We discuss how a "small & quiet pet" includes goldfish, clams, and "fruit" as listed on page 8 of the book; we add turtles, hamsters, guinea pigs, and birds to this list (although bird owners may argue about the quietness of their pets!). I transfer the information onto a sheet of butcher-block paper

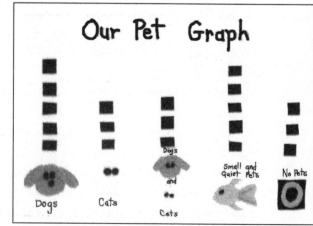

Our Pet Graph

and distribute 3-by-3-inch squares of black construction paper to students as markers for the graph.

I call on individuals to add personal pet information to the graph by attaching one or more markers in the appropriate space(s). For instance, George glued two markers onto the graph, one for his dog and one for his goldfish. Amanda added markers for the dog, the turtle, and the hamster living at her house.

After all the students have contributed information to the graph, I pass out grid paper and invite them to transfer the data from our class pet graph to this paper. Students draw animals for each type of pet and then color a box on the grid to represent each construction-paper marker on our pet graph.

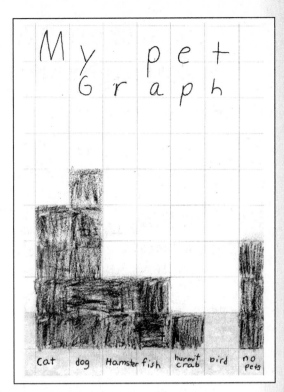

Maggie's Pet Graph

....

Crickwing
by Janell Cannon

 **Patterns**

One cockroach had looked like all the others—
until a close call with a hungry toad. In his wild
escape from the toad's sticky tongue, he had twisted
one of his fine long wings. Since then everyone
called him Crickwing.

— From *Crickwing*, page 5

This close call with a hungry toad left Crickwing in constant pain and very bitter. His only pleasure in life came from playing with his food; he took comfort in the bright colors and interesting shapes of leaves, roots, and petals, and built sculptures from the food before eating it.

Crickwing learns a lesson from a group of hardworking leaf-cutting ants who are much kinder than he. The ants go against their queen's orders and let Crickwing go free. This kindness causes a change of heart in Crickwing, who vows to help the leaf-cutters out of their predicament. Putting his food sculpting talent to good use, he creates his finest sculpture and wins the queen's respect as well as an invitation to join the colony.

> ## Rich Vocabulary
>
> **despised** *v.* disliked in a big way

The stunning illustrations and heartwarming tale make *Crickwing* a favorite read-aloud choice among second graders. Share this story, and then offer it for silent reading so students can get a closer one-on-one look at this must-have book.

Use *Crickwing* as a springboard to a math lesson on patterns. Display the book's cover. Talk about the designs Crickwing is making with the torn flower petals. Students surmise that, although a color pattern is not evident, there is definite planning going into the sculpture. Ask them to follow Crickwing's lead and make a 5-step pattern using torn paper of different colors. Display the patterns on a bulletin board reserved for such book-based activities. Provide time for students to discuss the creation of their patterns.

Jesse's 5-step *Crickwing* pattern

Cloudy with a Chance of Meatballs
by Judi Barrett

LEARNING ABOUT **Addition and Subtraction Word Problems**

What if you never had to go to the grocery store again because all your meals fell like rain from the sky? Aside from the convenience factor, not having a say in what's for dinner could become bothersome. And, as we discover in *Cloudy with a Chance of Meatballs*, getting three square meals a day this way becomes messy and downright dangerous. Read Judi and Ron Barrett's popular book to discover what happened in the town of Chewandswallow when the weather took a turn for the worse and the people had to abandon their homes—it became a matter of survival.

Following your read-aloud of the book, bring it to a math lesson for a zany book-based twist on 2-digit addition and subtraction word problems. Provide students with food-related manipulatives such as beans, dry pasta, and bottle or milk caps for hands-on help in solving the problems. Pass out place-value boards and small ketchup cups or empty yogurt containers for counting and regrouping tens and ones as needed. Plain white paper

Rich Vocabulary

prediction *n.*
a guess about what might happen

plates make great book-related recording sheets on which students can write the number sentences that describe each word problem.

Cloudy with a Chance of Meatballs Math

1. On Monday, partly cloudy skies dropped 11 meatballs onto Sandy's plate at lunch and 12 at dinner followed by a sprinkling of Parmesan cheese. How many meatballs did Sandy get all together on Monday? (11 + 12 = 23 meatballs)

2. On Tuesday, a warm front blew in blueberries on winds of 5 miles per hour. Molly collected an entire bucketful of blueberries and grabbed 2 handfuls before pouring the rest onto her pancakes. She ate 15 blueberries from one hand and 17 blueberries from the other. How many blueberries did she eat in all? (15 + 17 = 32 blueberries)

3. On Wednesday, the forecast called for a 90 percent chance of Tater Tots for lunch. Sam and Greg were going to have a Tater-Tots eating contest. They each had 2 bowls ready to catch the falling Tater Tots. After the storm, Sam had 32 Tater Tots in one bowl and 19 Tater Tots in the other. Greg had 29 Tater Tots in one bowl and 16 Tater Tots in the other. If they both ate all their Tater Tots, how many Tater Tots did each one eat? (Sam: 32 + 19 = 51 tater tots; Greg: 29 + 16 = 45 Tater Tots)

4. On Thursday, it drizzled brussels sprouts all day. Andrew counted 26 brussels sprouts in the bowl on his family's table. He fed 10 brussels sprouts to the dog. How many brussels sprouts were left? (26 − 10 = 16 brussels sprouts)

5. Friday brought a flurry of jellybeans. Cindy tucked 52 assorted flavors into her pockets. She ate all 12 of the grape jellybeans. How many jellybeans does Cindy have left? (52 − 12 = 40 jellybeans)

....

Alexander, Who Used to Be Rich Last Sunday
by Judith Viorst

 **Money**

It isn't fair that my brother Anthony has two dollars and three quarters and one dime and seven nickels and eighteen pennies.

It isn't fair that my brother Nicholas has one dollar and two quarters and five dimes and five nickels and thirteen pennies.

It isn't fair because what I've got is . . . bus tokens.

— From *Alexander, Who Used to Be Rich Last Sunday*, pages 5–7

> **Rich Vocabulary**
>
> **responsible** *adj.*
> able to do something

Poor Alexander. Saving money is hard for him. Alexander knows this because he used to be rich last Sunday—when his grandparents gave him a dollar. He buys gum, pays off a few debts, rents a snake, pays his dad for saying a few bad words and giving his brother a kick, and then spends his last 20 cents at a garage sale. Now all Alexander has left is bus tokens.

Prior to a math lesson on money, share *Alexander, Who Used to Be Rich Last Sunday* for read-aloud. Students will find Alexander's story comical while they sympathize with his money problems. Then let them spend some money of their own in a book-based math lesson about counting coins to one dollar—and prove just how quickly money disappears.

Provide groups of students with separate containers filled with pennies, nickels, dimes, and quarters (margarine tubs work well for this), and a stack of play one-dollar bills. As you reread the story, students manipulate the coins along with Alexander. On the first page of text, for instance, they count 2 dollars, 3 quarters, 1 dime, 7 nickels, and 18 pennies to find out how much money Anthony has. ($3.38) Then they count 1 dollar, 2 quarters, 5 dimes, 5 nickels, and 13 pennies to find out how much money Nicholas has. ($2.38)

When Alexander receives a dollar from his grandparents, have students take a dollar bill. As Alexander says goodbye to his first 15 cents, they exchange the bills for coins equal to a dollar. Then they part with 15 cents. Or you can have each student hand in a dollar bill and receive 85 cents in change.

With each turn of the page, Alexander loses more money until he is left with nothing but bus tokens—and the items he bought at the garage sale. As he parts with the different amounts of money, record them on a sales receipt. At the end of the lesson, ask students to add the different amounts to see if they really do add up to one whole dollar.

Sales Receipt for Alexander

  15 cents for gum
  15 cents in bets
  12 cents to rent snake
  10 cents for bad words
   8 cents flushed down toilet, fell through crack
  11 cents for Anthony's candy bar
   4 cents for Nick's magic trick
   5 cents for kicking brother
+ 20 cents at garage sale
  _____

  100 cents = 1 dollar

Ira Sleeps Over
by Bernard Waber

LEARNING ABOUT **Bar Graphs**

Ira is about to have his first sleepover at Reggie's house. Ira's so excited—until his sister reminds him that he's never slept without his teddy bear before. Now Ira is worried. What should he do? Take his teddy bear and risk being laughed at by Reggie? Or leave his teddy bear at home and be unable to sleep without it? Ira's parents say he should take the bear. Ira tries to ask Reggie his feelings about teddy bears, but Reggie keeps on talking about how much fun they'll have telling ghost stories. Ghost stories without his teddy bear? Now Ira is really worried about the sleepover.

This story about sleepover etiquette hits home with second graders who are at the age when many children, like Ira, attend their first sleepover. Share *Ira Sleeps Over* for read-aloud, and then use it as a springboard for making several different graphs. To introduce the read-aloud, briefly explain Ira's predicament and ask students to answer the following question by adding a learning link or a tally mark under Yes or No:

When Ira sleeps over at Reggie's house, should he take his teddy bear?

Yes	No
~~////~~ ~~////~~ ////	~~////~~ ///

Tally results, and take time to compare survey results with the actual ending of the story. Discuss the comical ending, and let children relate to Ira's feelings of concern and share similar personal experiences. Try a few other graphing ideas to get students constructing and interpreting graphs using the themes in *Ira Sleeps Over*. Here are some questions you might graph.

- Do you sleep with a teddy bear? Yes/No
- Ira has a sister. What is your place in the family?
  First and only child/First child/Second child/Third child/Fourth child
- How many hours do you sleep each night?
  Sunday/Monday/Tuesday/Wednesday/Thursday/Friday/Saturday
- At a sleepover, what would you like to do the most?
  Eat snacks/Go to sleep/Tell ghost stories/Have a pillow fight/
  Play a game

> ## Rich Vocabulary
>
> **dilemma** *n.* a problem that is hard to solve

Harry the Dirty Dog
by Gene Zion

Telling Time

*Harry was a white dog with black spots who liked everything,
except . . . getting a bath.
So one day when he heard the water running in the tub,
he took the scrubbing brush . . .
and buried it in the backyard.
Then he ran away from home.*

— From *Harry the Dirty Dog*, pages 5–7

Rich Vocabulary

furiously *adv.* with great effort, sometimes in an angry way

---

If dogs could have a hero, it would be Harry. Not many would go to the trouble that he does to avoid a bath. Like most dogs, Harry eventually became hungry, tired, and worried that his family might think he really has run away. So he swallows his pride and heads back over the fence. But Harry's family won't let him back in because they don't recognize the strange little dog in the backyard; after his playful day, Harry's no longer a white dog with black spots but a black dog with white spots. Being the problem solver that he is, Harry digs the scrubbing brush out of the backyard and rushes to the place he dislikes the most—the bathtub. His curious family follows. After the soapiest bath Harry has ever had, he becomes a white dog with black spots again.

Gene Zion's *Harry the Dirty Dog* has been entertaining young readers and their adults for nearly 50 years. In my second-grade classroom, students often share this book for student read-aloud and request it for silent reading time. When it's time for a lesson on telling time in 15-minute intervals, I use the events in Harry's day as inspiration. Prior to the lesson, I chart a few of the main events with a box for recording the time beside each event.

10:15	Harry hears water running in the tub.
10:30	Harry buries the scrubbing brush in the backyard.
	Harry plays where the street is being fixed.
	Harry plays at the railroad.
	Harry plays tag with his friends.
	Harry slides down a coal chute.
	Harry runs back home.
	Harry does some clever tricks.
	Harry dances and sings.
	Harry gets a bath.
	Harry gets combed and brushed.
	Harry has dinner.
	Harry falls asleep in his favorite spot.

Students make individual analog clocks from copies of the reproducible on page 94 (duplicated on heavy paper). Show them how to attach the hands to the clock with a paper fastener. Next, we gather for a lesson that assigns times in 15-minute intervals to Harry's day. Our lesson begins with the students setting their clocks to 10:15 as this is the time I designated for the first event, Harry hears water running in the tub. Fifteen minutes later, he's buried the scrubbing brush in the backyard. Students move the hands on their clocks to reflect the new time of 10:30. Ask a volunteer to share the time on his or her clock, and let the rest of the class compare it to their clocks. Continue with the rest of events, filling in the boxes as students tell you the times.

My Visit to the Aquarium
by Aliki

Water Habitats

TODAY I went to the aquarium with my little sister and my big brother.
The minute we walked in, I knew we'd have fun.
The aquarium is full of fish—and they are all alive!
Some of the fish—and other aquatic creatures—were born right here.
Some were collected from the salty seas and fresh waters where they live.
Here in the aquarium, they swim in their own kind of water,
in their own natural settings.
I found out how they live, just by looking.

— From *My Visit to the Aquarium*, page 5

Take your students on an outing to an aquarium by sharing *My Visit to the Aquarium* for read-aloud. Aliki Brandenburg presents a small boy as the narrator so students get a tour of the aquarium from a child's perspective and in appropriate second grade-language. As students go through the different exhibits in the aquarium, they learn facts in easy-to-remember, descriptive text that is accompanied by vivid illustrations.

The trip begins at the tropical coral reef that is "like a sunny under-water garden, busy with bright little fish." Eight pages later, the location is the giant kelp forest, "three stories high, and teeming with life." After feeding time, it's time to visit the shark tank, the tide pool creatures, and the muggy tropical rain forest. The freshwater exhibit is followed by the coastal stream exhibit where visitors view "fish that travel." The days ends with the biggest treat of all—the dolphins and beluga whales put on a show in their new pool.

Rich Vocabulary
thrive v. to do well or grow well
frolicked v. played happily

After your visit to the aquarium at read-aloud, share Aliki's message on page 33 where she lists alarming facts about the harm done to animals of the sea. She writes, "All the living things in this book are at risk. They are endangered by people who pollute, litter, and destroy the earth."

Use this book to introduce an activity where students can explore different water habitats by making a mural to remind people to protect our world. Divide the class into groups, and have them choose one of the following habitats to explore: tropical coral reef, deep sea, tide pool, coastal stream, and fresh water. Review *My Visit to the Aquarium* to point out reference pages for each group. Provide scrap paper, crayons, scissors, and glue sticks for students to create animals that live in their assigned habitats.

Have students attach the animals to blue butcher-block paper representing water. Or, if possible, have them use double-stick tape to attach ocean animals to windows in the classroom that have been covered with blue cellophane. Label each habitat mural, and add the title, "Protect Our World." These murals make a statement to visitors that your students are learning to do their part to care for the world that they share with creatures large and small.

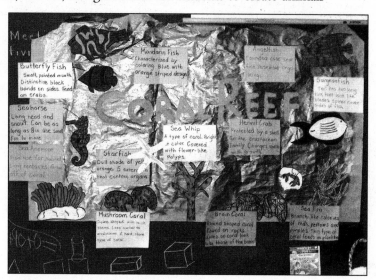

Our Window into the Tropical Coral Reef

The Wump World
by Bill Peet

LEARNING ABOUT

Protecting Earth's Resources

The Wumps were simple grass eaters and spent most of their time grazing on the tall tender grass that grew in the meadows. In warm weather they cooled themselves in the crystal-clear rivers and lakes. And at night they slept in the shelter of the bumbershoot trees to keep the dew off their backs.

— From *The Wump World*, page 2

If only the Wumps knew that someone a million miles away was watching their little world. The Pollutians from the planet Pollutus

Rich Vocabulary

timid *adj.* shy

wasteful *adj.* using more of something than is necessary

left their worn-out planet to begin again. Shortly after their spaceships landed on the Wump World, great cities sprang up. The Wumps were terrified and ran wild-eyed into the nearest cave where they feared they would have to spend the rest of their days avoiding the endless noise, smoke, and filth from the Pollutians.

Within a short amount of time, the Pollutians could no longer breath the air, drink the water, or stand the noise themselves. They abandoned the Wump World for yet another new land. When the world above them went silent, the Wumps came out of their hiding place. They were staggered by the damage to their beautiful, peaceful world, but they found hope in one remaining stretch of grassy meadow where they, too, could begin again—although they knew the Wump World would never be quite the same.

Share *The Wump World* for read-aloud on Earth Day during a study of animals and nature, or on any day you want to spread the word about doing our part to care for our world. Let master storyteller Bill Peet impress upon your students what can happen when pollution gets out of control and natural resources are wasted.

Make a list of things we can do to make a difference—from collecting trash on the playground to choosing products in recyclable containers, second graders can make a difference. Think about taking a field trip to a local park for a cleanup day in the spring. Make posters to display throughout the school or in the community as reminders to care for our Earth. As the Wumps discovered, we all have to work together now, or our world may never be quite the same.

· ·

Waiting for Wings
by Lois Ehlert

 **LEARNING ABOUT** **Life Cycles of Butterflies**

Out in the fields,
eggs are hidden from view,
clinging to leaves with butterfly glue.
Soon caterpillars hatch.
They creep and chew.
Each one knows what it must do:
Find a place where winds don't blow,
then make a case in which to grow.
— From *Waiting for Wings*, pages 4–11

The park near my house has a butterfly garden. Each spring, groups of first and second graders take field trips to the park and quietly walk the paths of the colorful garden as a culmination to their study of nature. As I walk my dogs along the outer path of the garden, I want to run home, grab my copy of *Waiting for Wings* and gather the children around me for read-aloud. Lois Ehlert has boldly and beautifully captured the excitement of what it's like to wait with anticipation for a butterfly to light on a flower that's been planted in its honor.

Butterfly garden field trip or not, this book begs to be shared in the spring during a study of nature or insects or on a blustery cold day when you and your students need a reminder of the promise of spring. The beautiful collage illustrations and rhyming text will brighten any day.

Then use *Waiting for Wings* to introduce students to the different stages from egg to butterfly. The informative pages at the back of the book are a great reference for butterfly identification and information, flower identification, and tips for growing a butterfly garden. As Lois Ehlert suggests, "Try to think like a butterfly . . ." Her book certainly helps readers do just that!

If possible, take students on a field trip to a butterfly garden so they can feel the anticipation of waiting for wings, too. If that's not possible, take them out to the playground and let them pretend to be waiting for butterflies. They'll get a sense of anticipation, and you may get a few moments of much needed silence!

Even More Must-Have Books as Springboards to Math and Science

Just a Dream by Chris Van Allsburg

The Great Kapok Tree by Lynne Cherry

Verdi by Janell Cannon

Pinkerton Behave by Steven Kellogg

Big Bad Bruce by Bill Peet

Me and the Measure of Things by Joan Sweeney

Jumanji: Math Game

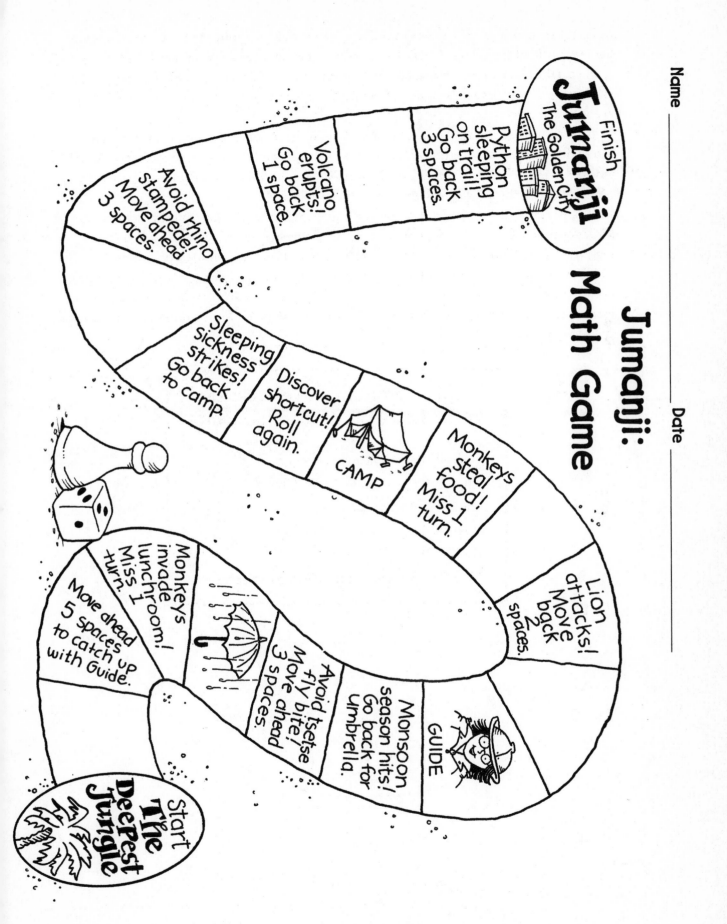

Finish
Jumanji
The Golden City

Python sleeping on trail! Go back 3 spaces.

Volcano erupts! Go back 1 space.

Avoid rhino stampede! Move ahead 3 spaces.

Sleeping Sickness strikes! Go back to camp.

Discover shortcut! Roll again.

CAMP

Monkeys steal food! Miss 1 turn.

Lion attacks! Move back 2 spaces.

Monsoon season hits! Go back for Umbrella.

GUIDE

Avoid tsetse fly bite! Move ahead 3 spaces.

Monkeys invade lunchroom! Miss 1 turn.

Move ahead 5 spaces to catch up with Guide.

Start
The Deepest Jungle

Use with Jumanji by Chris Van Allsburg • Teaching With Favorite Read-Alouds in Second Grade

Harry's Clock

Directions: Cut out the clock and the hour and minute hands.
Then attach the hands to the clock with a paper fastener.

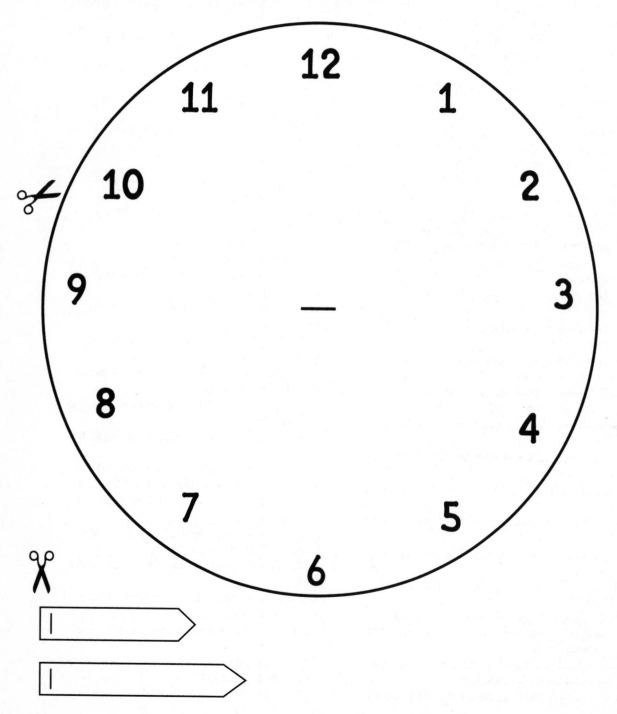

Use with Harry the Dirty Dog by Gene Zion • Teaching With Favorite Read-Alouds in Second Grade

50 Must-Have Books for Second Grade

Allard, Harry. *Miss Nelson Is Missing!* Houghton Mifflin Company, 1977.

Barrett, Judi. *Cloudy with a Chance of Meatballs.* New York: Aladdin Paperbacks, 1978.

Brandenberg, Aliki. *My Visit to the Aquarium.* New York: Harper Collins, Publishers, 1993.

Brett, Jan. *Berlioz the Bear.* New York: G. P. Putnam's Sons, 1991.

———. *Goldilocks and the Three Bears.* New York: The Putnam & Grosset Group, 1987.

———. *Town Mouse, Country Mouse.* New York: G.P. Putnam's Sons, 1994.

Brown, Marc. *Arthur's First Sleepover.* Boston: Little, Brown & Company, 1994.

Bunting, Eve. *The Wednesday Surprise.* New York: Clarion Books.

Burningham, John. *Hey! Get Off Our Train.* New York: Crown Publishers, Inc., 1989.

Cannon, Janell. *Crickwing.* Orlando: Harcourt, Inc., 2000.

Carle, Eric. *"Slowly, Slowly, Slowly," Said the Sloth.* New York: Philomel Books, 2002.

Cronin, Doreen. *Giggle, Giggle, Quack.* New York: Simon & Schuster Books for Young Readers, 2002.

dePaola, Tomie. *Strega Nona.* New York: Aladdin Paperbacks, 1975.

Ehlert, Lois. *Waiting For Wings.* Orlando: Harcourt, Inc., 2001.

Henkes, Kevin. *Chester's Way.* New York: Viking Penguin, 1988.

Hest, Amy. *When Jessie Came Across the Sea.* Cambridge, MA: Candlewick Press, 1997.

Huck, Charlotte. *Princess Furball.* New York: Greenwillow Books, 1989.

Isadora, Rachel. *Sophie Skates.* New York: G. P. Putnam's Sons, 1999.

Karlin, Barbara. *Cinderella.* Boston: Little, Brown, and Company, 1989.

Kellogg, Steven. *Chicken Little.* New York: Morrow Junior Books, 1985.

———. *A Rose for Pinkerton.* New York: Dial Books for Young Readers, 1981.

Lester, Helen. *Tacky the Penguin.* Boston: Houghton Mifflin Company, 1988.

Lobel, Arnold. *Frog and Toad Together.* New York: HarperCollins, 1971.

Marshall, James. *George and Martha: The Complete Stories of Two Best Friends.* Boston: Houghton Mifflin Company, 1997.

———. *Goldilocks and the Three Bears.* New York: Dial Books for Young Readers, 1988.

———. *The Three Little Pigs.* New York: Dial Books for Young Readers, 1989.

Martin, Bill, Jr. and Archambault, John. *Barn Dance!* New York: Henry Holt and Company, 1986.

MacLachlan, Patricia. *All the Places to Love.* New York: HarperCollins Children's Books, 1994.

Nixon, Joan Lowery. *If You Were a Writer.* New York: Aladdin Paperbacks, 1988.

Peet, Bill. *The Wump World.* Boston: Houghton Mifflin Company, 1970.

Pilkey, Dav. *Dragon Gets By.* New York: Orchard Books, 1991.

———. *'Twas the Night Before Thanksgiving.* New York: Orchard Books, 1990.

Plourde, Lynn. *Pigs in the Mud in the Middle of the Rud.* New York: Blue Sky Press, 1997.

Polacco, Patricia. *My Rotten Redheaded Older Brother.* New York: Simon & Schuster Books for Young Readers, 1994.

Prelutsky, Jack. *It's Raining Pigs and Noodles.* New York: Greenwillow Books, 2000.

Rylant, Cynthia. *The Great Gracie Chase.* New York: The Blue Sky Press, 2001.

———. *Henry and Mudge Take the Big Test.* New York: Bradbury Press, 1991.

Scieszka, Jon. *The Frog Prince Continued.* New York: Viking Penguin, 1991.

———. *The True Story of the 3 Little Pigs!* New York: Viking Penguin, 1989.

Steig, William. *The Amazing Bone.* New York: Farrar, Straus, Giroux, 1976.

———. *Sylvester and the Magic Pebble.* New York: Simon and Schuster, Inc. 1969.

St. George, Judith. *So You Want to Be President.* New York: Philomel Books, 2000.

Van Allsburg, Chris. *Jumanji.* Boston: Houghton Mifflin Company, 1981.

Viorst, Judith. *Alexander, Who Used to Be Rich Last Sunday.* New York: Aladdin Paperbacks, 1978.

Waber, Bernard. *Ira Sleeps Over.* New York: Houghton Mifflin Company, 1972.

———. *Lyle, Lyle, Crocodile.* Boston: Houghton Mifflin Company, 1965.

Wells, Rosemary. *Bunny Cakes.* New York: Puffin Books, 1997.

———. *Fritz and the Mess Fairy.* New York: Dial Books for Young Readers, 1991.

Young, Ed. *Lon Po Po.* New York: Putnam Publishing Group, 1996.

Zion, Gene. *Harry the Dirty Dog.* New York: Harper and Row, Publishers, Inc., 1956.

Grade 2 Learning Skills

Reading with fluency and expression
Barn Dance!, p. 31
Hey! Get Off Our Train, p. 33
Miss Nelson Is Missing!, p. 38
Pigs in the Mud in the Middle of the Rud, pp. 39–40
'Twas the Night Before Thanksgiving, p. 32

Reading strategies
Cause and effect:
Chicken Little, pp. 66–67
Making comparisons:
Princess Furball, pp. 68–69
Making inferences:
Frog and Toad Together, p. 35
The True Story of the 3 Little Pigs!, pp. 65–66
Making predictions:
Lon Po Po, pp. 69–70
Retelling a story:
Giggle, Giggle, Quack, p. 36
Self-correction:
Dragon Gets By, p. 37
Sequence:
Frog and Toad Together, p. 35
'Twas the Night Before Thanksgiving, p. 32

Story Elements
Goldilocks and the Three Bears, pp. 60–63
Strega Nona, pp. 71–72
Characters and events:
Cinderella, p. 68
The Three Little Pigs, p. 64
Theme:
The Frog Prince Continued, pp. 70–71

Writing in a variety of genres
Captions:
Sophie Skates, pp. 52–53
Journaling:
The Wednesday Surprise, pp. 57–58
Letters:
"Slowly, Slowly, Slowly," Said the Sloth, pp. 44–47

Newspaper articles:
Berlioz the Bear, pp. 55–56
Personal experience:
Chester's Way, pp. 19–20
My Rotten Redheaded Older Brother, pp. 49–50
Place description:
All the Places to Love, pp. 51–52
Speeches:
So You Want to Be President, pp. 55–56

Writing process
If You Were a Writer, pp. 48–49

Adjectives
Fritz and the Mess Fairy, pp. 22–23

Capitalization
George and Martha: The Complete Stories of Two Best Friends, pp. 14–16

Punctuation
George and Martha: The Complete Stories of Two Best Friends, pp. 14–16
Miss Nelson Is Missing!, p. 38

Spelling conventions
Arthur's First Sleepover, pp. 17–18
Bunny Cakes, pp. 16–17
Chester's Way, pp. 19–20
Town Mouse, Country Mouse, pp. 13–14

Syllables
It's Raining Pigs and Noodles, pp. 26–30

Vowel Sounds
Long vowel sounds:
The Great Gracie Chase, pp. 21–22
Short vowel sounds:
Tacky the Penguin, pp. 18–19

Vocabulary awareness
Descriptive language:
When Jessie Came Across the Sea, pp. 54–55

Rhyming words:
It's Raining Pigs and Noodles, pp. 26–30
Word endings:
Lyle, Lyle, Crocodile, pp. 20–21
Sylvester and the Magic Pebble, pp. 8–12
Synonyms:
The Amazing Bone, pp. 53–54
Word recognition:
Henry and Mudge Take the Big Test, pp. 34–35

MATH
Addition and subtraction
Cloudy with a Chance of Meatballs, pp. 84–85

Graphs
A Rose for Pinkerton, pp. 82–83
Ira Sleeps Over, p. 87

Money
Alexander, Who Used to Be Rich Last Sunday, pp. 85–86

Number relationships
Jumanji, pp. 77–81

Patterns
Crickwing, pp. 83–84

Time
Harry the Dirty Dog, pp. 88–89

Word problems
Cloudy with a Chance of Meatballs, pp. 84–85

SCIENCE
Earth's resources
The Wump World, pp. 90–91

Living things
Butterflies:
Waiting for Wings, pp. 91–92

Water habitats
My Visit to the Aquarium, pp. 89–90